ArtStarts
For Little Hands!

WILLIAMSON ®
Little Hands

Library of Congress Cataloging-in-Publication Data

Press, Judy, 1944-
   ArtStarts for Little Hands!: fun & discoveries for
3- to 7-year-olds / by Judy Press.
      p. cm. — (A Williamson Little Hands book)
      Includes index.

   Summary: Presents a variety of art projects and
   related activities grouped around such themes
   as animals, nature, transportation, color,
   and more.
      ISBN 1-885593-37-6
      1. Art—Study and teaching (Elementary)
      2. Project method in teaching. [1. Art—
      Technique. 2. Handicraft.] I. Title. II. Series.

   N350 .P73 2000
   372.5'044—dc21   99-089956

Little Hands® series editor: **Susan Williamson**
Project editor: **Emily Stetson**
Cover design: **Trezzo-Braren Studio**
Interior design: **Pisaza Design Studio, Ltd.**
Illustrations: **Karol Kaminski**
Printing: **Capital City Press**

Little Hands®, *Kids Can!*®, *Kaleidoscope Kids*®, and
Tales Alive!® are registered trademarks of Williamson
Publishing Company. *Good Times!*™ and *Quick
Starts*™ *for Kids!* are trademarks of Williamson
Publishing Company.

Williamson Publishing Co.
P.O. Box 185
Charlotte, Vermont 05445
1-800-234-8791

Manufactured in the United States of America

10 9 8 7 6 5 4 3 2

Dedication

For Anaëlle,
avec tout mon amour.

Acknowledgments

I would like to thank the following for their support and
encouragement in the writing of this book: Carol Baicker-
McKee and Andrea Perry; the Mt. Lebanon Public Library
and its children's librarians; my husband, Allan, and my
children, Debbie, Darren, Matthew, Brian, and Aliza.

This book would not have been possible without the talent
and dedication of the following people at Williamson
Publishing: Susan and Jack Williamson, Emily Stetson, June
Roelle, Vicky Congdon, Jean Silveira, and Merietta McKenzie.
A special thanks to Joe Borzetta and Patricia Isaza at Pisaza
Design Studio, Ltd.; illustrator Karol Kaminski; and Ken
Braren and Loretta Trezzo at Trezzo-Braren Studio for their
creative talents.

A Williamson *Little Hands*® Book

ArtStarts
For Little Hands!

Fun & Discoveries for 3- to 7-Year-Olds

By Judy Press

Illustrations by Karol Kaminski

WILLIAMSON PUBLISHING • CHARLOTTE, VERMONT

CONTENTS

For Grown-Ups   vi
It All Starts with Art!   viii

Animal Friends   **1**

Terrific Turtles   2
Kitty Cat   4
Bird in a Cage   6
Cuckoo Bird Mask   8
School of Fish   10
Easy Elephant   12
Brown Bear Puppet   14
Salt Clay Mouse   16

A Sunny Day   **19**

Super Sailboats   20
Runaway Balloons   22
Goofy Glasses   24
Tissue-Paper Sun Catchers   26
Sandy Island   28
Sunshine Wand   30
Perky Hat   32

Away We Go!   **35**

Key Ring   36
Back-Seat Drivers   38
Bus Ride   40
In the Car   42
Stop & Go!   44
Racing Cars   46
Circus Train   48
Choo-Choo Train   50

Color Starts   **53**

Colorful Circles   54
Popsicle Stick Match   56
Color Sort   58
Rainbow Mobile   60
Colored Puzzle Shapes   62
Pinwheel Color Spin   64
Color Spin Game   66

In My Garden — 69

Lovely Ladybugs — 70

Funny Flower — 72

Flying Paper Bird — 74

The Carrot Patch — 76

Apple Tree — 78

Spider Web — 80

Fluttering Butterfly — 82

Nighttime Fun — 85

Blinking Fireflies — 86

Stencil Stars — 88

My Bedtime Book — 90

Silvery Moon — 92

Winter Fun — 95

Matching Mittens — 96

Snowy Pine Tree Mobile — 98

Snowy Footprints — 100

Snowy Day Scene — 102

Fluffy Snowman — 104

Learning Fun — 107

Mix Up, Match Up — 108

Lace-Up Shoes — 110

Playful Puppets — 112

Tick-Tock Clock — 114

Music Shaker — 116

Activity Index By Skill Level — 118

For Grown-Ups

Art has tremendous value in its own right to the child in us all. It provides an open avenue for expression of emotions, fantasies, and the specifics of time and place in our personal small worlds.

But early art experiences for the very young child are important in so many additional ways that we are just beginning to appreciate. Yes, the dynamic, creative process of art is a truly wonderful way for young children to express themselves; with that we all agree. But the artistic process also builds a strong foundation in specific developmental areas: motor skills, color and shape recognition, sorting, categorizing and sequencing, listening and dramatic play, social skills and cooperative play.

Over many years of sharing art with children, I have developed art activities that teach and support basic academic skills for pre-reading and pre-writing readiness (word recognition, visual and tactile discrimination, and the development of fine and gross motor skills); mathematics (symmetry, patterns, geometric shapes, numbers, and sequences); and

science (observation of plant and animal life, sensory awareness, and weather/climate concepts). Indoor and outdoor activities, books to read, and games to play are included here as well, to help children experience learning as an ongoing process without limits of time, place, subject, or particular materials.

It's Child's Play!

Although specific instructions are provided for each project, always allow the child to make choices and follow his or her own muse. Avoid holding up perfectly completed projects that will only intimidate and stifle creativity. Instead, present varied, child-made projects using the themes and supplies at hand. The message should be clear: The possibilities are endless! Encourage new ideas, fanciful designs, and individualized interpretations so that each piece of art reflects the creativity and mood of the child who made it. Most of us need to remind ourselves that the experience of creating is more important than the finished product.

Encourage lots of chatter and conversation as the children work. Sometimes a reluctant artist will lose self-consciousness if the room feels alive with conversation, humming, and kids working where they feel comfortable — at desks, tables, and on the floor.

Safety First!

One of the first personal safety rules is never to force a child to participate. Some kids just don't feel inspired or are shy. Suggest something else to do, such as looking at books or quietly observing others. The art experience is very personal; we need to respect even the youngest artist's personal boundaries.

Always plan for different ability levels, offering help to those who need it to get beyond a difficult spot. Fine motor skills develop at each child's own rate, so using scissors or gluing smaller pieces on may be simple for one child and extremely difficult for another. To avoid frustrating a child, be ready to help and then quickly put the creativity back into the child's hands. And remember that helping means cutting or attaching — not redoing or improving upon what the child has done!

Check the skill level (1, 2, or 3) to get an idea of the relative skill level involved in each project. And for beginners, go to the Simpler ArtStarts; for more advanced artists, go to the More ArtStarts — both in the Learning Connections section that accompanies each activity.

Of course, always work in a well-ventilated room with nontoxic materials. Assess your young artists' propensity to put small objects in their mouths. Children younger than two still regularly suck on things, so be very, very careful. Keep in mind, too, that younger siblings may pick up odds and ends from the floor or pull items off the table's edge. Clean-up should be thorough.

Please note: Paper fasteners used in some of the crafts in this book can present a choking and poking hazard. I suggest that you keep the fasteners in your pocket and put them on each project as needed. Do not leave them in a dish on the table.

The materials needed to create the art projects are readily available; many are recycled paper products. Where scissors are used, please use child safety scissors — it's worth it to invest in a pair that can really cut. Provide guidance with tools such as staplers and hole punches as needed, too.

Most important, maintain a relaxed, fun, and lively atmosphere where a good time can be had by all. *ArtStarts for Little Hands!* is written for children and the grown-ups in their lives. Use this opportunity to spend time together and share in the joy of creating and the excitement of learning!

It All Starts with Art!

Art is fun
    to explore,
But look again
    and you'll learn more.

Let's count with art —
    me and you!
Two apples are red,
    three birds are blue!

Let's look for shapes,
    they're everywhere.
Wheels are round,
    a block is square!

Let's close our eyes,
    then touch and feel.

There's fuzzy felt,
    and cars of steel!

Let's gather things
    that we can sort.
Some crayons are long
    and some are short!

Let's play with clay
    and make a ball.
The first one's large,
    the next one's small!

So go ahead
    let's learn with art,
'cause now's the perfect
    time to start!

Terrific Turtles

One, two, three!
How many turtles do you see?
Look! Two for you,
One for me!

What You Need

- **Child safety scissors**
- **Styrofoam tray (from fruits or vegetables)**
- **Pencil with dull point**
- **White tempera paint, in dish or lid**
- **Green or brown construction paper**
- **Black marker**

What You Do

Draw

1. Cut out a large oval from the center of the tray. Pressing down hard, draw a design into the oval.

2. Dip the oval design into the paint; press, paint side down, onto the paper. Repeat to make more turtle designs. Allow to dry.

3. Use the black marker to outline each turtle's shell, head, legs, eyes, and tail. Wow! Did you make a pattern of turtles?

Dip

Outline

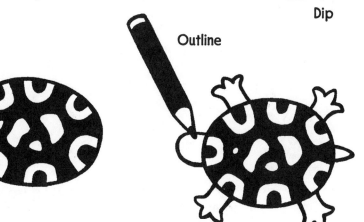

Learning Connections

Simpler ArtStarts

Cut around the corners of a kitchen sponge for an oval shape. Dip the sponge into a thin layer of tempera paint and press onto the paper for a turtle's shell. Let dry. Use a marker to draw on the turtle's head, legs, and tail.

With My Friends

Have a turtle race. Drape a pillow across your back, and get on your hands and knees. Line up side by side. Then, at the sound of "Go," begin the race. The first "turtle" to cross the finish line wins.

Math Starts

Print five turtles; cut them out. Number each turtle. Now, spread the turtles, number side down, on a table. Turn the turtles over one at a time, placing them in order until the numbers appear one after another from lowest to highest or highest to lowest.

Kitty Cat

Kitty likes to
take a nap,
curled up tightly
on my lap.

What You Need

- **Child safety scissors**
- **Small white paper plates, 2**
- **Kitchen sponge**
- **Black tempera paint, in dish or lid**
- **Black and red markers**
- **Paper fastener***
- **White craft glue**
- **Wiggly eyes**

***Note:** Paper fasteners pose choking and poking danger to young children. Adults should control the supply and insert them into the project.

What You Do

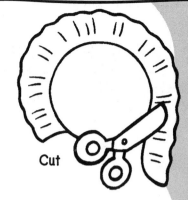
Cut

1. Cut off the rim of the first paper plate. From the rim scraps, cut out the cat's ears, paws, and tail. Use the center of the plate for the cat's head.

2. Dip the sponge into the black paint and press onto the cat's ears, paws, tail, and head and the entire second plate. Allow to dry.

Sponge-paint

3. Use the black marker to draw the cat's whiskers and claws, and to outline the head, tail, ears, eyes, and body. Use the red marker for the cat's mouth and nose.

4. Ask a grown-up to poke a hole through the whole paper plate and tail. Attach the tail with a paper fastener. Glue on the cat's face, paws, ears, and wiggly eyes. Now, move the tail back and forth.

Outline

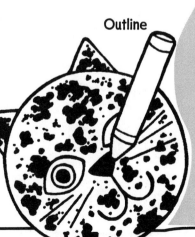

Learning Connections

Simpler ArtStarts

Collect cotton balls, felt, feathers, yarn, and other soft materials. Glue them onto cardboard to make a collage that's kitty-soft!

Dramatic Play

Pretend you're a cat. Crouch in the center of your room and close your eyes. What senses can you use to help you "see?" Describe the smell of things in the room. What can you learn by touching things? Can you carefully find your way around the room, using your outstretched arms and hands?

Story Time

Read the book *Mrs. Katz and Tush* by Patricia Polacco. Do you know a cat? What would you name your own cat?

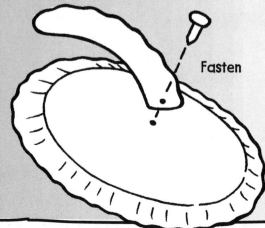
Fasten

Bird in a Cage

Some fine feathered friends
are flying your way;
Make them a home
where they can stay!

What You  Need

- **Child safety scissors**
- **Clear plastic drinking straw**
- **Pipe cleaners, 2**
- **Marker**
- **Yellow construction paper**
- **Tape**
- **Plastic berry baskets, 2**

Make perch

Simpler ArtStarts

Dip the bottom of a berry basket in a thin layer of tempera paint. Press the basket onto paper for a basket-weave print. For added fun, paste bird images from magazines onto the basket prints.

1. Cut off a third of the straw. To make a perch, pass one pipe cleaner stem through the short straw section. Cut the second pipe cleaner into four 2" (5-cm) pieces.

Tape bird

More ArtStarts

Make a home zoo, using other berry baskets as cages for pretend pets. Make salt-clay (see page 18) animals to place in each basket with some paper-strip bedding. Secure the baskets with twist-ties. *Grrr ...*

2. Draw a bird on the yellow paper. Cut it out and tape it to the perch.

3. Turn the berry basket upside down. Hang the perch from the center of the basket. Place the basket with the perch on top of the second basket. Twist pieces of pipe cleaner through to hold the baskets together.

Nature Starts

Do you "eat like a bird"? Birds like to eat berries, raisins, peanut butter, and sunflower seeds — all good kid snacks, too! Slather peanut butter on a piece of cereal-box cardboard and press on some seeds. Hang with yarn in a tree for a bird-loving treat!

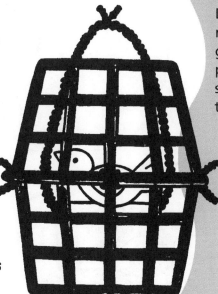

Fasten baskets

Cuckoo Bird Mask

The cuckoo bird
Sticks out its head,
And tells the children
"Time for bed!"

What You Need

- **Child safety scissors**
- **Paper cups, 2**
- **Brown construction paper**
- **Tape**
- **White craft glue**
- **Craft feathers, 2**
- **Markers**
- **Stapler**
- **Elastic band**

What You Do

1. Cut the tops off the paper cups, leaving a 1" (2.5-cm) section around the bottom. Cut out a hole in the center of each cup for the bird's eyes.

2. Cut a 5" x 5" (12.5-cm x 12.5-cm) construction-paper square. Cut a fan shape across one corner of the square; fold into a cone and tape to hold.

3. Tape the bird's eyes together; tape the cone below the eyes. Glue feathers on top and decorate eyes with markers if desired.

4. Ask a grown-up to staple or tie an elastic to the outside edge of each cup. Adjust so elastic fits. Now, act like a cuckoo clock, you cuckoo bird!

Cut cups

Fold & tape

Tape

Decorate & add elastic

Learning Connections

Simpler ArtStarts

Draw a bird on construction paper; glue on artificial feathers. Blow on the feathers like a gentle wind.

Song & Dance

Sing "Hickory, Dickory, Dock." You and your friends can be the mouse. How would you show, while standing in one spot, the mouse running up the clock, and coming down?

Nature Starts

The cuckoo is just one of many kinds of birds. How many different kinds of birds can you name? Look in a bird identification book with a grown-up to see all the different kinds of birds that live near you.

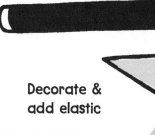

School of Fish

When schools of fish
swim in the sea
They keep each other
company!

- Cardboard tube
- Large white paper plate
- Black tempera paint, in dish or lid
- Markers (green, black, and other colors)
- Blue crayon

What You Do

1. Press the cardboard tube flat, to form an oval shape at the end. Dip the end of the tube in the paint; press onto the plate. Repeat the design to make six fish. Allow to dry.

2. Use the black marker to draw each fish's tail, eyes, and gills. Use the green marker for seaweed. Color three fish one color, and the rest another color. Lightly rub the blue crayon around the fish for water.

Repeat design

Color

LEARNING Connections

Simpler ArtStarts

Cut out fish from different wrapping papers. Arrange them in groups, called *schools*. Glue the fish onto blue construction paper.

Sorting Fun

Did you put all of your fish together by color? If you did, then you are a sorter! See if you can sort the crayons in the crayon box by color or size. Then, ask if you can help sort the laundry or a pile of socks.

With My Friends

Tie a string to the end of a long pole. Tie a magnet to the string. Cut out some paper fish. Attach a paper clip to each fish. Put all the fish in a shallow box and see how many fish each player can "catch."

Story Time

Read *The Rainbow Fish* by Marcus Pfister. Talk about how the Rainbow Fish's feelings changed in the story. Do your feelings sometimes change, too?

*Note: Paper fasteners pose choking and poking danger to young children. Adults should control the supply and supervise use.

Easy Elephant

Big ears, a trunk —
What can it be?
Is that an elephant
that I see?

What You Need

- **Child safety scissors**
- **Large white paper plate**
- **Gray crayon**
- **White or gray construction paper, 2 sheets**
- **Tape**

What You Do

1. Cut the paper plate in half for the elephant's ears. Color them gray.

2. Cut a band of construction paper to fit around your head. Fold it over on itself the long way; tape the ends together. Color with crayon to match the ears.

3. Cut a slit in one corner of each ear. Slide the ears onto the headband. Tape to hold.

4. To make the trunk, fold the second sheet of paper the long way, making a tube; color and tape together. Tape the trunk to the headband.

Cut

Tape

Make trunk

Learning Connections

Simpler ArtStarts

Cut a small white paper plate in half. Tape to the sides of a large white paper plate. Color the plates gray. Cut out eyeholes and tape a paper trunk to the large plate for an elephant mask.

Motor Skill Fun Starts

An elephant's trunk can pick up things that are large and small — such as tree trunks and berries! Put your hand in a sock for a pretend trunk. How many large and small things can you pick up?

Dramatic Play

Pretend you're an elephant. Hold your hands together and extend your arms out in front for a trunk. Move around the room with slow, stomping footsteps. Do you think you'd like to be a real elephant?

Brown Bear Puppet

Brown bear climbing
up a tree,
Don't get stung
by a honeybee!

What You Need

- **Child safety scissors**

- **White paper plates,
  1 large & 1 small**

- **Brown crayon**

- **Tape**

- **Brown paper lunch bag**

- **Paper fastener***

- **White craft glue**

- **Wiggly eyes**

- **Brown, black, and red markers**

What You Do

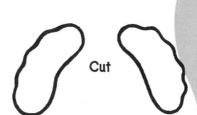

Cut

Tape

1. Cut out the bear's nose from the center of the small paper plate. Cut away the rim from the large plate to make the head; cut out paws and ears from the rim. Color the bear pieces brown.

2. Put the small circle on top of the large circle. Ask a grown-up to poke a hole through the centers; attach to the flap of the bag with a paper fastener. Tape the bear's paws to the edge of the flap and the ears to the top of the large circle.

3. Glue on the wiggly eyes. Use the markers to draw the bear's mouth, eyebrows, and bow tie. Put your hand inside the bag to make the bear move.

Glue

Music Starts

Put on a bear parade. Invite your friends to bring along their stuffed bears. March and parade to music, holding your bears high.

Dramatic Play

Use bear puppets to act out the story of *The Three Bears* with three friends. Crouch down behind the back of the couch for your puppet theater. "Ladies and Gentlemen, the Little Hands Puppet Theater presents ..."

Story Time

Read the book *Brown Bear, Brown Bear, What Do You See?* by Bill Martin. Then, sitting in a circle with some friends, hold up a stuffed bear and ask, "Little bear, little bear, what do you see?" Describe something in the room, without naming it. The other players look around the room and try to guess what it is. The player who guesses right gets to be the next to describe something.

*Note: Paper fasteners pose choking and poking danger to young children. Adults should control the supply and insert them into the project.

Salt Clay Mouse

Little mice
in gray or white,
Scamper through
the house at night.

What You Need

- Salt clay (see recipe, page 18)
- Old metal tablespoon
- Cookie sheet
- Black, red, and white tempera paint, in dishes or lids
- Paper plate, for mixing colors
- Thin paintbrush

What You Do

Press clay into spoon

1. Press a lump of clay into the spoon for a mouse body. Gently pull the clay along the spoon's handle for a tail.

2. Roll tiny balls of clay for eyes, nose, and ears; press them into the rounded mouse body.

Make eyes, nose & ears

3. Place the mouse — still in the spoon — on a cookie sheet. Ask a grown-up to bake the clay until hardened in oven, or allow to air-dry. Then, carefully slide the clay mouse off the spoon.

4. Mix some black and white paint to paint the mouse gray; mix red and white paint for a pink nose. Add black details for the eyes and ears.

Bake

Learning Connections

Simpler ArtStarts

Shape the salt clay into a ball (body); flatten slightly. Roll a small piece of clay into a long thin snake (tail) and press into body. Press small stones or beans on for the mouse's eyes, nose, and ears. Allow to air-dry.

More ArtStarts

Make a mouse family using different sizes of spoons, such as a serving spoon, a soup spoon, and a teaspoon. Compare their sizes. Paint them different colors.

Math Starts

Animals come in all shapes and sizes, some even *smaller* than a tiny mouse and *bigger* than an elephant. Cut out pictures of animals from old magazines. Glue your collection onto paper, starting with the *smallest* animal you find and ending with the *biggest*.

With My Friends

Play Cat & Mouse. Hold hands to form a circle with the "cat" and the "mouse" outside the circle. The cat chases the mouse. You help the mouse by lifting your arms up to let it in or out, trying to keep the cat away. Once the mouse is caught, play again with a new cat and mouse.

SALT CLAY

1 1/2 cups (375 ml) salt
4 cups (1 L) flour
1 1/2 cups (375 ml) water

1. Mix the dry ingredients together in a plastic bowl; add water.
2. When dough forms a ball around the spoon, knead the dough well, adding water if it is too crumbly. Once the clay holds together, it's ready to be molded.
3. Allow molded clay to air-dry or bake in a 300°F (150°C) oven for 30 to 40 minutes, or until hard.

Super Sailboats

Boats with their sails
hoisted high;
Reds, yellows, blues,
floating by.

What You Need

- **White craft glue, in a small dish or lid**
- **Styrofoam plate**
- **Paintbrush**
- **Blue tissue paper**
- **Child safety scissors**
- **Egg carton**
- **Construction paper**
- **Toothpicks**

Glue

1. Mix a few drops of water into the glue. Turn the plate upside down and brush the glue mixture over the bottom. Press the tissue paper into the glue on the plate. Brush more glue over the paper. Let dry.

2. To make boats, cut out four sections from the egg carton. To make sails, cut eight triangles from construction paper (two for each boat). Glue a toothpick mast between every two triangles. Let dry.

3. Glue the egg-carton boats onto the tissue-covered plate. Poke the toothpick masts through each boat and into the plate.

Cut

Build

Learning Connections

Simpler ArtStarts

Cut out triangle shapes from different colors of construction paper. Glue triangles onto blue paper for sails. Use markers to draw on the boats' masts and hulls.

Math Starts

For a boat race, number each sail. Be the announcer, calling out the number of the boat that is in the lead. What number boat is coming in second? Which boat is in last place?

More ArtStarts

Rinse, dry, and open the spout end on any size milk carton. Ask a grown-up to help cut the carton in half the long way. Re-form the remaining spout and staple closed for a boat. Then, try it out in a tub or sink full of water!*

Science Starts

Fill a basin with water. Add floating leaves, plastic deli lids, a cork, recycled aluminum foil, pebbles, and quarters to the basin. What floats like a boat? What sinks to the bottom? Do you have more sinkers or floaters?

Note: Even a shallow basin of water poses a drowning threat to a toddler. Never leave a toddler unattended near any amount of water.

Runaway Balloons

Colorful balloons
in the sky;
Gently drifting
Way up high.

What You Need

- **Child safety scissors**
- **Small white paper plates, 3**
- **Crayons, 3 colors**
- **Tape**
- **String**
- **Glue stick**
- **Blue construction paper**
- **Cereal-box or shirt cardboard**
- **Self-sticking Velcro dots**

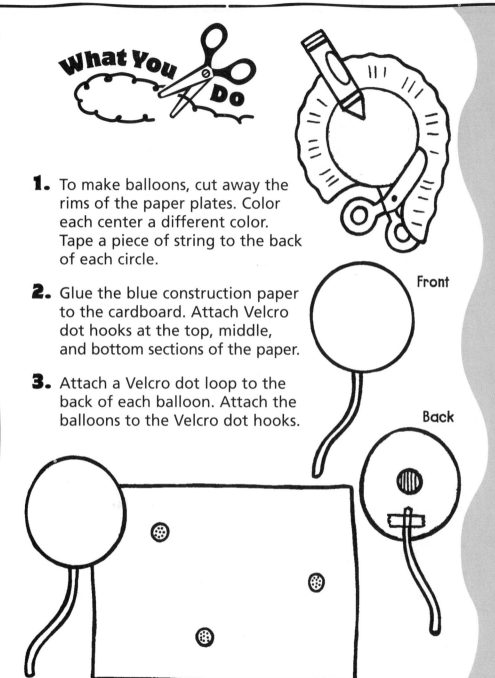

What You Do

1. To make balloons, cut away the rims of the paper plates. Color each center a different color. Tape a piece of string to the back of each circle.

2. Glue the blue construction paper to the cardboard. Attach Velcro dot hooks at the top, middle, and bottom sections of the paper.

3. Attach a Velcro dot loop to the back of each balloon. Attach the balloons to the Velcro dot hooks.

Front

Back

LEARNING Connections

Simpler ArtStarts

Cut out balloons from different colors of construction paper. Glue the balloons onto blue construction paper. Use a black marker to draw strings.

More ArtStarts

Make a larger balloon poster, with seven removable balloons. Write the names of the days of the week, one per balloon. Mix them up; then put them back in order!

Hi-Lo

Move the balloons to different positions on the paper. Which color balloon is now the *highest*? The *lowest*? In the *middle*?

Dance

Put on some soft music. Pretend to be a balloon, floating up toward the sky on tiptoes with your arms raised up high. What happens when a wind comes up?

Goofy Glasses

These glasses are
such fun to wear;
Why not make
an extra pair?

What You Need

- **Clear plastic yogurt-sized lids, 2**
- **Pipe cleaners, 2 plus a short extra piece**
- **Colored plastic wrap**
- **Child safety scissors**

 **What You Do**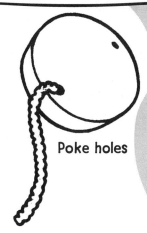

Poke holes

1. Ask a grown-up to poke a hole on both sides of each plastic lid. Hold the lids side by side. Twist the short piece of pipe cleaner through the two inner holes for the eyeglass bridge piece.

2. Twist the two long pipe cleaners through each of the two outer holes. Bend the ends of the pipe cleaners to fit around your ears.

3. Cut plastic wrap to fit inside the lids. Press the wrap in place with your fingers.

4. Try on your shades!

Cut

LEARNING Connections

Simpler ArtStarts

Cut out the center of a small paper plate. Lay colored plastic wrap across the opening; tape to hold. Tape a Popsicle stick to the bottom of the plate. Now, hold your sunglasses by the stick and peek through.

More ArtStarts

Decorate your sun specs with glitter, tissue paper, ribbons, and flowers. Make them as funny or as beautiful as you feel today.

Creative Thinking

How does the world look through your colored glasses? Does everything look prettier? Funny? Scary? Better?

Story Time

Read the book *One Hot Summer Day* by Nina Crews.

Science Starts

Keep a record of the week's weather. Draw seven large squares on paper, one for each day of the week. Each day, check the weather outside and draw on a symbol that describes the weather best (like a sun, clouds, umbrella, snowflake). What symbol can you use for a windy day?

Tissue-Paper Sun Catchers

The sun shone bright
But just till noon.
Did someone chase it
Away too soon?

What You Need

- **White craft glue**
- **Styrofoam tray (from fruits or vegetables**
- **Paintbrush**
- **Tissue paper, several colors**
- **Child safety scissors**
- **Hole punch**
- **Ribbon**

What You Do

1. Mix the glue with a few drops of water in the bottom of the tray. Spread out the glue mixture with the paintbrush.

2. Tear off pieces of tissue paper and press into the glue. Continue layering the tissue in the glue until the bottom of the tray is covered and each piece of tissue is moist with the glue mixture. Allow to dry overnight.

3. Peel the sheet of tissue off the tray. Use scissors to cut out tissue-paper shapes you like. Punch a hole in the top of each shape and thread with ribbon. Hang the suncatchers in a window.

Mix glue; layer tissue paper

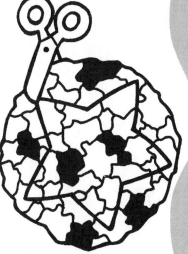

Cut shapes

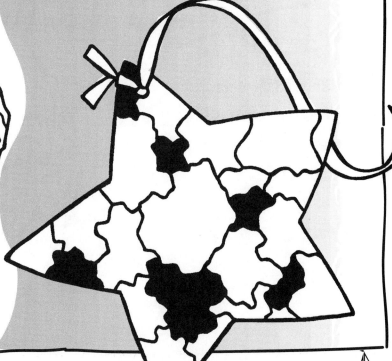

LEARNING Connections

Simpler ArtStarts

Stick scraps of tissue paper onto the sticky side of clear contact paper. Lay another piece of clear contact paper over the top. Cut the contact paper into a shape. Punch a hole in the top of the shape and hang with yarn.

More ArtStarts

Use permanent markers to draw designs on clear plastic deli lids. Punch a hole in the top and hang from ribbon or yarn.

Sandy Island

Toes in the mud,
hands in the sand;
Cool tickling water
touches the land.

What You Need

- **White paper plate**
- **Green and blue markers**
- **Child safety scissors**
- **Sandpaper**
- **White craft glue**
- **Old magazines or stickers**

What You Do

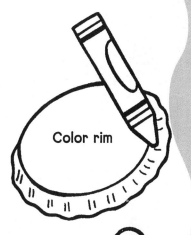

Color rim

1. Turn the paper plate upside down. Color the rim blue and green for ocean waves.

2. Cut the sandpaper to fit inside the rim of the plate, and glue on for a sandy beach.

3. Cut out pictures of sea life from magazines or use stickers. Glue on the island or in the water, as appropriate.

Cut the sandpaper

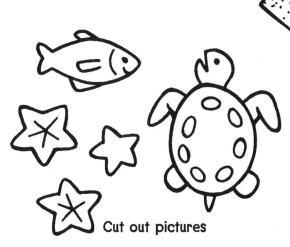

Cut out pictures

LEARNING Connections

Simpler ArtStarts

Glue sandpaper onto blue construction paper. Glue stickers of fish and seashells around the sandpaper.

Science Starts

Cut out pictures of creatures that live in the water, creatures that live on land, and creatures that seem to live in both places (like an alligator). How do you think an animal can breathe on land and in the water, too?

Story Creations

Dictate a story to a grown-up or on a tape recorder about an imaginary day at the beach. Did you meet a wonderful sea creature or find a treasure?

Sunshine Wand

Hello, Mr. Sun!
You're looking bright.
When you're high in the sky
The day's just right!

What You Need

- **Red, orange, and yellow construction paper**
- **Paper-towel tube**
- **Tape**
- **Small paper plate**
- **White craft glue**

1. Wrap a sheet of construction paper around the paper tube. Tape to hold.

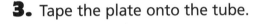

Wrap

2. Tear construction paper into long, thin strips. Glue the strips onto the paper plate, so that the "rays" hang off the side.

3. Tape the plate onto the tube.

Tear

Tape

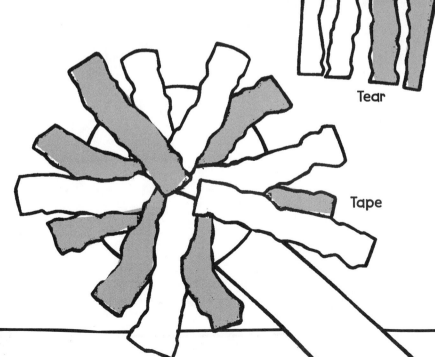

Simpler ArtStarts

Color a small paper plate with yellow and orange crayons or markers to look like the sun. Tape the plate to a paper-towel tube.

Story Creations

People of long ago talked to the rising sun. They told stories to explain how the sun had come to be. Make up your own story about how the sun came to shine in the sky every day. Draw pictures to illustrate your sun tale.

With My Friends

Plan a sunrise picnic with a grown-up. Check the newspaper the day before to see exactly when the sun will rise. Then, set your alarm clock for a little earlier. Bring a picnic breakfast, a jacket, and a flashlight. Head for a place to view the sunrise. Wow! It's beau-ti-ful!

More ArtStarts

Lay flat objects such as keys, paper cutouts, and combs on dark-colored construction paper. Leave the paper in direct sun (at noon is best) on a bright, sunny day. Place a rock in each corner of the paper to hold it in place. After four or five hours, pick up the objects to see your sun print. Now how did that happen?

Perky Hat

Hats for cold,
hats for sun,
Make this hat
just for fun!

- **Masking tape**
- **Fuzzy towel**
- **Large white paper plate**
- **Crayons, several colors**
- **Child safety scissors**
- **Stapler**
- **Ribbon**

1. Press strips of tape onto a fuzzy towel; then, lift them off. (This makes the tape less sticky.)

2. Lay the tape in a pattern — or at random — around the paper plate. Color over the entire plate with crayons.

3. Lift up the strips of tape to reveal the "uncolored" pattern.

4. Make a cut from the outside edge of the paper plate into the center. Overlap the edges, forming a peak, and staple the slit ends together. Staple a ribbon or ties to the sides of the hat.

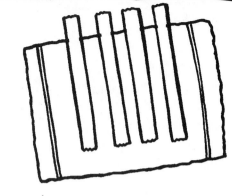

Press tape onto towel

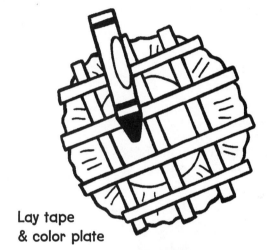

Lay tape & color plate

Cut

Overlap & staple

Simpler ArtStarts

Use markers to color a large white paper plate. Attach a ribbon to the sides of the plate for a quick and colorful sun hat.

More ArtStarts

Press fuzzy tape onto paper in the shape of letters or words. Use crayons to color over and around the tape. Lift up tape and you'll have colorful letter designs!

Sort & Group

Cut out hats from some old magazines. Sort the hats into summer hats and winter hats, or big hats and little hats. Glue them onto a piece of newspaper to make gift wrap. Pick out one special hat that you like best and paste it on a picture of YOU!

Story Time

Read *Hats, Hats, Hats* by Ann Morris, *The 500 Hats of Bartholomew Cubbins* by Dr. Suess, and *Caps for Sale* by Esphyr Slobodkina. Can you name three types of workers who wear special hats to work?

Key Ring

When Mom and Dad
can't find their keys,
Give them this ring —
It's sure to please!

What You Need

- Pencil
- Keys
- Construction paper, assorted colors
- Child safety scissors
- Hole punch
- Markers
- Pipe cleaner

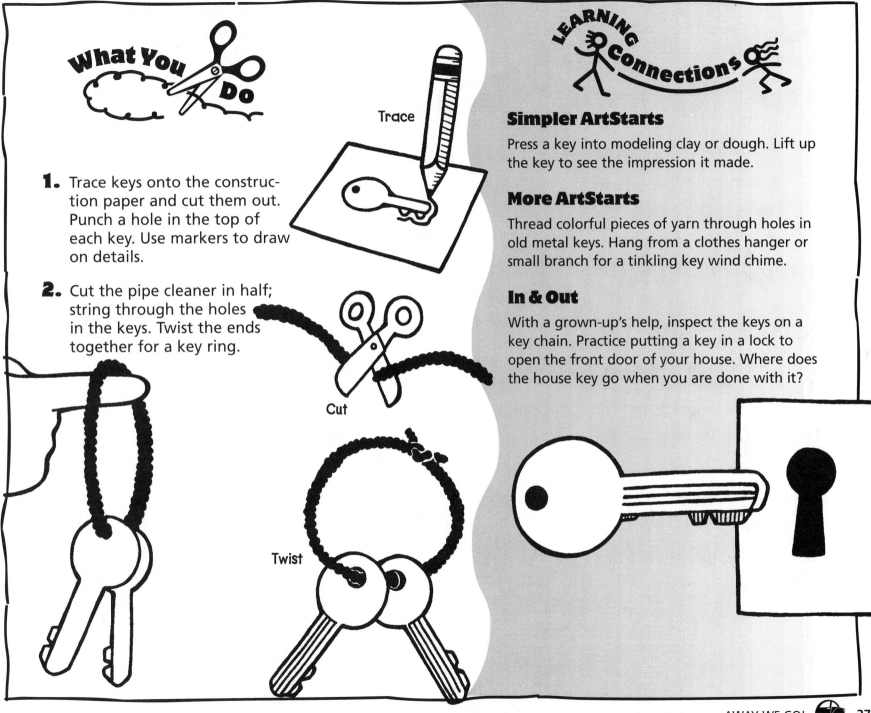

What You Do

1. Trace keys onto the construction paper and cut them out. Punch a hole in the top of each key. Use markers to draw on details.

2. Cut the pipe cleaner in half; string through the holes in the keys. Twist the ends together for a key ring.

Trace

Cut

Twist

LEARNING Connections

Simpler ArtStarts

Press a key into modeling clay or dough. Lift up the key to see the impression it made.

More ArtStarts

Thread colorful pieces of yarn through holes in old metal keys. Hang from a clothes hanger or small branch for a tinkling key wind chime.

In & Out

With a grown-up's help, inspect the keys on a key chain. Practice putting a key in a lock to open the front door of your house. Where does the house key go when you are done with it?

Back-Seat Drivers

A car, a driver,
passengers, too;
Buckling up is
the first thing we do!

What You Need

- **Markers**
- **White business-sized envelope**
- **Child safety scissors**
- **Glue stick**
- **Black construction-paper scrap**
- **Old magazines or photos**
- **Cereal-box cardboard**

Cut

Glue

1. Draw a large car, with front and rear windows, onto a white envelope. Cut out the car's rear window (but don't cut out the back of the envelope). Glue the envelope shut.

2. Cut out two tires from the black paper. Glue onto the bottom of the envelope.

3. Cut out faces from magazines or old photos. Glue a face in the car's front window.

4. Cut out a 2" x 12" (5- x 30-cm) strip from the cardboard. Then, glue some faces onto the cardboard strip, starting 1" (2.5 cm) in from one end and spacing faces about 1" (2.5 cm) apart.

5. Cut a slit in both ends of the envelope wide enough for the cardboard strip. Now, pull those back-seat drivers through!

Simpler ArtStarts

Cut out a large car from a magazine. Cut out a face from an old photo. Glue the face in the window of the car.

Color & Size Sort

Arrange toy cars and trucks by color and size. How many cars are blue? How many are yellow? Which are small? Which are large? Which one do you like best?

Shape & Color ID

Cut out a window in the center of a white paper plate. Cut a slit on either side of the window. Cut out a slip of paper wide enough to fit through the slits. Draw shapes and colors across the paper; then, feed it through the slit to name the shapes and colors as they appear! Great job!

More ArtStarts

Cut a strip of construction paper 2" (5 cm) wide that fits around your wrist. Cut out pictures of you and your friends and glue them across the strip. Cover the strip with clear contact paper. Close with a hook-and-loop fastener to make a special friendship bracelet!

Bus Ride

Take a bus
into town,
Climb the hills,
then coast down!

- **Child safety scissors**
- **Egg carton**
- **Wooden ice-cream spoons, 8**
- **Markers**
- **Yellow construction paper**
- **Paper clips**

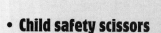

SCHOOL BUS

What You Do

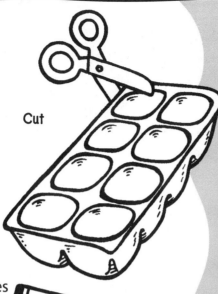

Cut

1. Cut away four sections from one end of the egg carton, so you have eight sections left. Turn the carton upside down. Poke a slit in each section.

2. To make passengers, draw faces on the wooden spoons. Place each passenger, with face outward, into a slit.

Draw

3. Fold the yellow paper in half. Draw windows on both halves and cut them out. Draw wheels underneath the windows.

4. "Tent" the yellow paper over the egg carton. Attach the paper to the carton with paper clips.*

Note: Paper clips pose a choking danger to young children. An adult should control the supply and supervise use.

Learning Connections

Simpler ArtStarts

Draw faces on wooden ice-cream spoons. Cut slits in a sheet of shirt cardboard. Insert the spoons into the slits. Draw the outline of a bus around the spoons.

Number Match-Up

Number each passenger and each section of egg carton. When it's time for the passengers to get on, place them in their matching seats.

Dramatic Play

Sing "The Wheels on the Bus" and act out the song using hand motions.

In the Car

In the car
on a sunny day,
See the sights
passing your way!

 **What You Need**

- **Large white paper plates, 2**
- **Child safety scissors**
- **Markers**
- **Scenic road pictures from old magazines, 2**
- **Tape**
- **Paper fastener***

***Note:** Paper fasteners pose choking and poking danger to young children. Adults should control the supply and insert them into the project.

What You Do

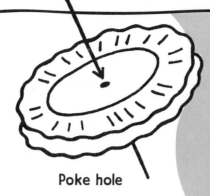

Poke hole

1. Lay the plates inside each other. Ask a grown-up to poke a hole through the center of both plates.

2. Cut out a windshield from inside one of the paper plates. Draw a steering wheel below the windshield.

Draw

3. Turn the other plate upside down. Tape a scenic picture on the top half. Then turn the plate around and tape a second picture on the bottom half.

4. Attach the plates back to back with a paper fastener. Turn the top plate to see different scenes through the windshield.

Fasten

LEARNING Connections

Play & Learn

Play an ABC game the next time you go for a ride in the car: A grown-up calls out a letter of the alphabet and players look for that letter in signs along the road. When a player finds the letter, he or she calls it out. Then on to the next letter.

With My Friends

Cut out a STOP sign from red construction paper. The leader shouts a direction, such as, "Stamp your feet" or "Turn to the right." Players continue the motion until the leader holds up the stop sign. The first person to stop becomes the next leader.

Stop & Go!

Red light, green light
Yellow light, too!
When you see these colors
Do you know what to do?

What You Need

- **Pencil**

- **Lids from deli containers, 3**

- **Red, yellow, green, and black construction paper**

- **Child safety scissors**

- **Tacky glue**

- **Paper-towel tube**

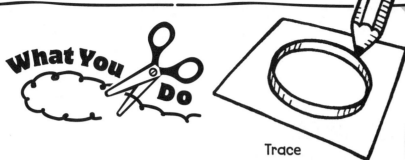

What You Do

Trace

1. Trace a deli lid onto the green, yellow, and red construction paper. Trace the lid twice on the black paper.

2. Cut out the paper circles so they fit snugly inside the lids.

3. Glue the lids onto the cardboard tube: the red lid on top, the yellow lid in the middle, and the green lid on the bottom. To make each color turn "on," place black circles over the other two colors, so only one color shows.

Cut

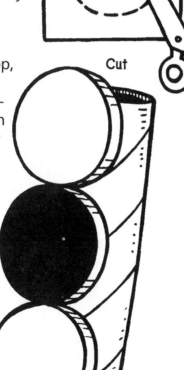

LEARNING Connections

Simpler ArtStarts

Paint three small white paper plates: one red, one yellow, and one green. Glue the plates onto black construction paper to make a traffic light.

More ArtStarts

Glue deli container traffic lights onto a sheet of cereal-box cardboard. Make a sign at the top, such as "Justin's Room." Tape the stoplight to the outside of the door. Use the black paper circles to indicate which light is on: Green for "Come In," red for "Please Stay Out," and yellow for "Knock First."

Rules of the Road

What three things do you do when you're crossing the road with a grown-up? That's right — you stop, look, and listen! Make up a rhyme using those three words.

With My Friends

Play Red Light, Green Light. Players stand two car lengths behind the leader. The leader turns her back, closes her eyes, and shouts, "Green light!" as she counts to 10. All players move forward and try to tag the leader before she turns around and shouts, "Red light!" Players caught moving must turn back. The first player to reach the leader

Racing Cars

Hotrods race
to the finish line,
Hooray! The winning car
is mine!

What You Need

- **Child safety scissors**
- **Styrofoam egg carton**
- **Permanent black marker**
- **Small stickers or colored tape**
- **White paper plates, 1 large & 1 small**
- **Black tempera paint, in lid or dish**
- **Paintbrush**
- **Toothpicks**
- **Tape**
- **Paper fastener***

***Note:** Paper fasteners pose choking and poking danger to young children. Adults should control the supply and insert them into the project.

What You Do

Cut

1. To make race cars, cut out six sections from the egg carton, trimming each around the sides. Draw on windows and doors. Put a different sticker, strip of tape, or number on top of each car.

Draw

2. Cut away the rim from the small paper plate. Paint the top of the plate black, leaving the outer edge white. Turn the large paper plate upside down and paint the bottom black, leaving an edge of the rim white. Let dry.

Cut & paint

3. Poke a toothpick through the sides of each car. Tape the other end of the toothpick under the small plate.

4. Ask a grown-up to poke a hole in the center of both plates. Attach the plates with a paper fastener. Turn the top plate to start the race.

Paint & tape

Simpler ArtStarts

Poke a hole in the center of a small paper plate and attach it to a large upside-down plate with a paper fastener. Use markers to draw colorful cars around the edge of the small plate. Turn the small plate to race the cars.

With My Friends

Draw a two-lane racetrack on a large sheet of poster board. Color one lane red; the other black. Divide lanes into equal sections. Place a toy car on each lane. Draw a card from a face-down deck of playing cards. If it's red, move the car on the red track forward as many sections as the number on the card (jacks, queens, and kings count as 1). If the card is black, move the car on the black track ahead. The first car to circle the track is the winner.

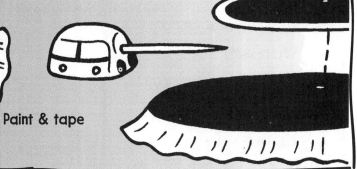

Circus Train

Elephants, acrobats,
popcorn, and clowns;
The circus train
is coming to town!

What You Need

- **Cardboard milk carton, 1 quart size (1 L)**
- **Masking tape**
- **Pencil**
- **Construction paper, assorted colors**
- **Child safety scissors**
- **White craft glue**
- **Animal pictures or stickers**
- **Toothpicks**
- **Markers**

Tape

MILK

1. Flatten the spout end of the carton. Tape to hold.

2. Trace the side of the carton four times onto construction paper. Cut out and glue to the carton.

GLUE

3. Glue or stick animal pictures onto the covered carton. Glue toothpicks over the pictures to make cage bars. Let dry.

4. Decorate the circus car with markers.

GLUE

Decorate

LEARNING Connections

Simpler ArtStarts

Glue animal pictures onto construction paper. Use markers to enclose the animals.

More ArtStarts

Make a circus-train bank. Slit the top of the car for a coin slot; open the spout to count your change!

Math Starts

Make more circus cars. Count the number of animals on your circus train. Which car has the most animals?

Story Time

Read a book about the circus, such as *Emeline at the Circus* by Marjorie Priceman. Or find out how Curious George saves the act at the circus in *Curious George Rides a Bike* by H. A. Rey. Make popcorn with a grown-up and pour it into a paper cone for a circus snack!

Dramatic Play

Draw an animal mask on a large paper plate. Tie it on with yarn strung through hole punches on either side. Then, form a circus train with your friends, placing your arms on the shoulders of the player in front of you. Don't let go or a wild animal may escape!

Choo-Choo Train

The train is coming!
Clickety, clack.
It leaves in the morning
and then comes back!

What You Need

- Index cards, 4" x 6" (10 x 15 cm)
- Transparent tape
- Hole punch
- Child safety scissors
- Paper fasteners*
- Cardboard egg carton
- Markers

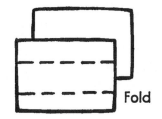
Fold

To make the cars

1. Hold two index cards the long way; fold each one into thirds.

2. Place one card upside down inside the second card; tape to hold together.

3. Make more train cars by folding and taping additional index cards. Punch a hole in the ends of each car.

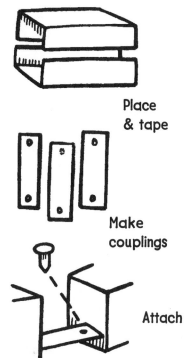
Place & tape

Make couplings

Attach

To make the couplings

1. Cut out 1" x 3" (2.5- x 7.5-cm) rectangles from another index card.

2. Punch a hole in the ends of each strip.

3. Attach couplings between the train cars with paper fasteners*.

To make the engine

1. Cut out one section of the egg carton. Holding the index card vertically, tent it over the egg section; tape to hold.

2. Tape the engine car to the first train car.

Use markers to decorate the train and draw on wheels.

*Note: Paper fasteners pose choking and poking danger to young children. Adults should control the supply and insert them into the project.

Simpler ArtStarts

Glue index cards end to end onto construction paper to make a train. Draw on windows and wheels.

Math Starts

Number the index card cars in order from *lowest* to *highest*. Uncouple the cars; then, couple them back together going from *highest* to *lowest*.

Dramatic Play

Line up a row of chairs. The engineer sits in the first chair and calls out, "All Aboard!" Kids add sound effects such as *choo-choo, chug-chug, whoo-whoo*. At each "stop," one chair (car) is removed, the engineer gets off, and the next person moves up to the engineer's seat.

Story Time

Read the books *Freight Train* by Donald Crews, *Smokey* by Bill Peet, or *The Little Engine That Could* by Watty Piper.

Finger Play & Song

Sing "Down at the Station" and act out the words with motions.

Down at the station, early in the morning

See the little puffabillies all in a row.

See the station master pull the little handle

Puff, puff, toot, toot! Off they go!

Color Starts

Colorful Circles

Look for circles,
Here's what you'll spy:
A bouncing ball,
A wheel, a pie!

What You Need

- **White tempera paint**
- **Styrofoam tray, from fruits or vegetables**
- **Round objects (paper cup, tube, bottle cap, spool, button, washer)**
- **Construction paper, assorted colors**
- **Child safety scissors**
- **Glue stick**

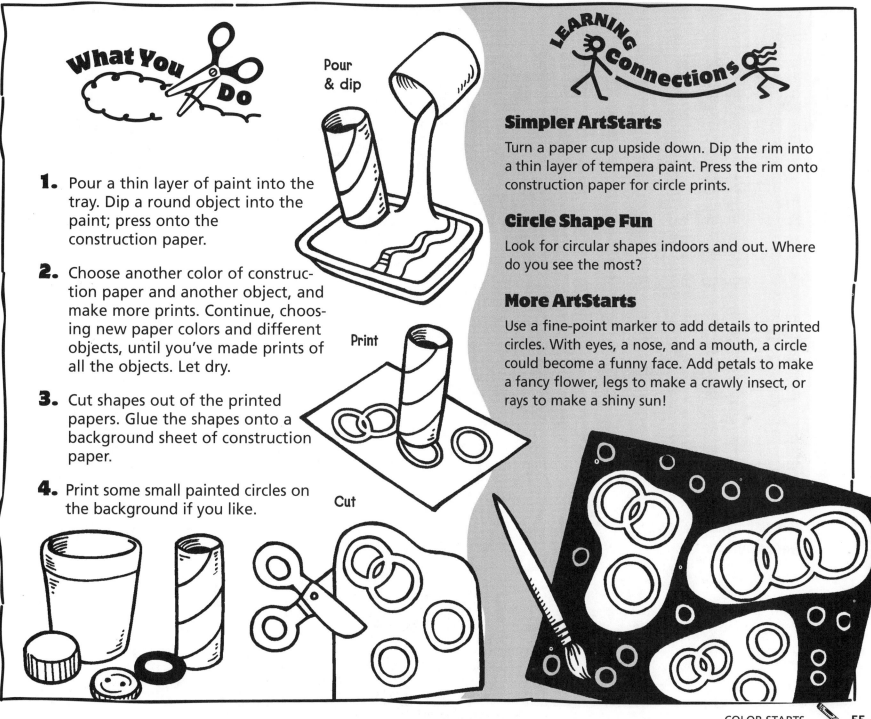

What You Do

1. Pour a thin layer of paint into the tray. Dip a round object into the paint; press onto the construction paper.

2. Choose another color of construction paper and another object, and make more prints. Continue, choosing new paper colors and different objects, until you've made prints of all the objects. Let dry.

3. Cut shapes out of the printed papers. Glue the shapes onto a background sheet of construction paper.

4. Print some small painted circles on the background if you like.

Pour & dip

Print

Cut

Learning Connections

Simpler ArtStarts

Turn a paper cup upside down. Dip the rim into a thin layer of tempera paint. Press the rim onto construction paper for circle prints.

Circle Shape Fun

Look for circular shapes indoors and out. Where do you see the most?

More ArtStarts

Use a fine-point marker to add details to printed circles. With eyes, a nose, and a mouth, a circle could become a funny face. Add petals to make a fancy flower, legs to make a crawly insect, or rays to make a shiny sun!

Popsicle Stick Match

Popsicle sticks all in a row. Color and count them as you go!

What You Need

- **White paper**
- **Popsicle sticks, 10**
- **Pencil**
- **Red, yellow, blue, and green markers**

What You Do

1. Starting at one end of the paper, trace one Popsicle stick. Leave a space. Now trace two Popsicle sticks next to each other. Next, trace three sticks and then four next to each other.

2. Color the real Popsicle sticks: one yellow, two red, three green, and four blue.

3. Color in the stick tracings: one yellow, two red, three green, and four blue.

4. Match up the sticks to the color strips.

Trace

Color

Match

With My Friends

Turn Pospsicle Stick Match into a game. Take turns picking a stick and placing it on the correct picture, matching the colors.

Simpler ArtStarts

Use markers to color Popsicle sticks: one yellow, two red, three green, and four blue. Group Popsicle sticks together by color.

Math Starts

Stack five sheets of construction paper together. Staple down one side to make a book. Decorate the cover with the numbers 1, 2, 3, and 4. Cut out pictures from old magazines and glue them into the book in *sets* from one to four, such as one smiling face, or four shoes.

Count-It Scavenger Hunt

Outdoors, look for one flower, two acorns or nuts, three rocks, and four leaves. Indoors, look for one shoe, two socks, three spoons, and four crayons.

COLOR STARTS **57**

Color Sort

Sorting colors
One by one.
Come and help us;
Please join the fun!

What You Need

- **White business-sized envelopes, 2**
- **Child safety scissors**
- **Construction paper**
- **Glue stick**
- **Markers, 4 colors**
- **Old magazines and catalogs**

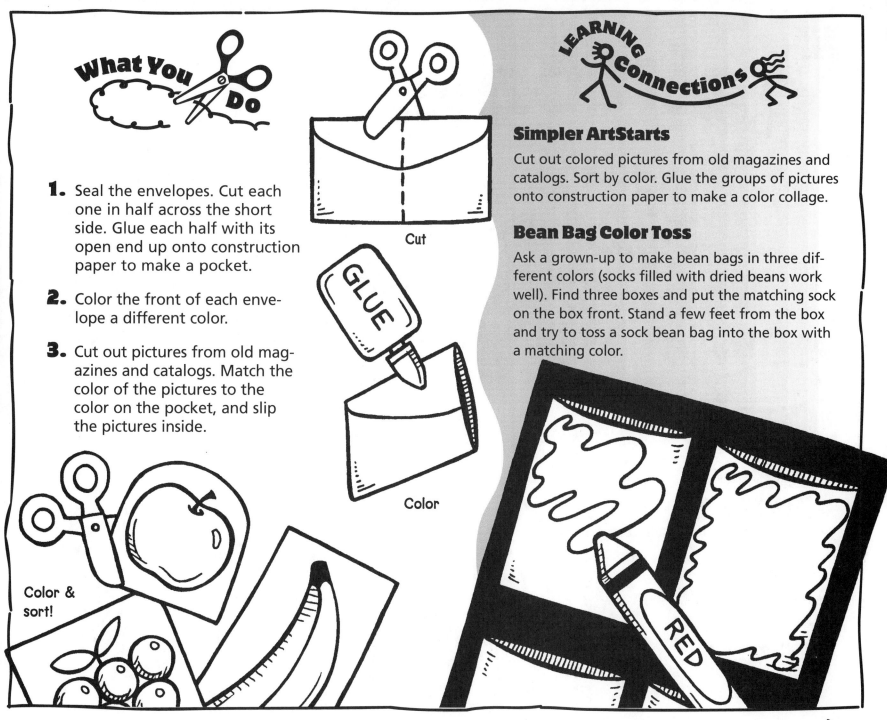

What You Do

1. Seal the envelopes. Cut each one in half across the short side. Glue each half with its open end up onto construction paper to make a pocket.

2. Color the front of each envelope a different color.

3. Cut out pictures from old magazines and catalogs. Match the color of the pictures to the color on the pocket, and slip the pictures inside.

Cut

GLUE

Color

Color & sort!

LEARNING Connections

Simpler ArtStarts

Cut out colored pictures from old magazines and catalogs. Sort by color. Glue the groups of pictures onto construction paper to make a color collage.

Bean Bag Color Toss

Ask a grown-up to make bean bags in three different colors (socks filled with dried beans work well). Find three boxes and put the matching sock on the box front. Stand a few feet from the box and try to toss a sock bean bag into the box with a matching color.

RED

Rainbow Mobile

Can you see the rainbow colors
where you live?
Can you name the rainbow colors?
ROY G. BIV!

What You Need

- **Child safety scissors**
- **Large paper plate**
- **Watercolor paints**
- **Paintbrush and water container**
- **Hole punch**
- **Plastic drinking straw**
- **Thin yarn, 2 strands**
- **White craft glue**
- **Cotton balls**

Paint & hang rainbow

1. Cut away the rim of the paper plate. Cut the center of the plate in half.

2. Use watercolors to paint a rainbow on both sides of one half. Punch a hole in the top of the rainbow.

3. Cut the straw in half. Thread the yarn through the hole in the rainbow and tie it to the center of the straw.

4. Cut out two clouds from the other half of the paper plate. Punch a hole in the top of each cloud. Glue cotton balls onto both sides of each cloud.

Cut & glue

5. Thread the other piece of yarn* through the straw with grown-up help, so that the ends hang down. Tie a cloud to each yarn end. Tie yarn around the middle of the straw to hang the mobile.

*Hint: To make yarn easy to thread, soak it in white craft glue and let dry.

LEARNING Connections

Simpler ArtStarts

Spread several colors of finger paint across wet paper to make a rainbow.

Rainbow Colors

Have you ever seen a rainbow? The colors are always in exactly the same order: **R**ed, **O**range, **Y**ellow, **G**reen, **B**lue, **I**ndigo (a shade of blue), and **V**iolet (purple). They spell the pretend name of ROY G. BIV!

Rainbow Friendship Chain

Make a rainbow chain with six friends. Cut strips of red, orange, yellow, green, blue, indigo, and purple construction paper. Each person gets one color. Join together to make a paper chain, in the order of the colors of the rainbow, taping strips to hold.

Story Time

Read *Planting a Rainbow* by Lois Ehlert.

Colored Puzzle Shapes

Puzzles are pictures and works of art. They fit together and come apart!

What You Need

- Child safety scissors
- Red, blue, and yellow construction paper
- Pencil
- Shirt or cereal-box cardboard
- Tape

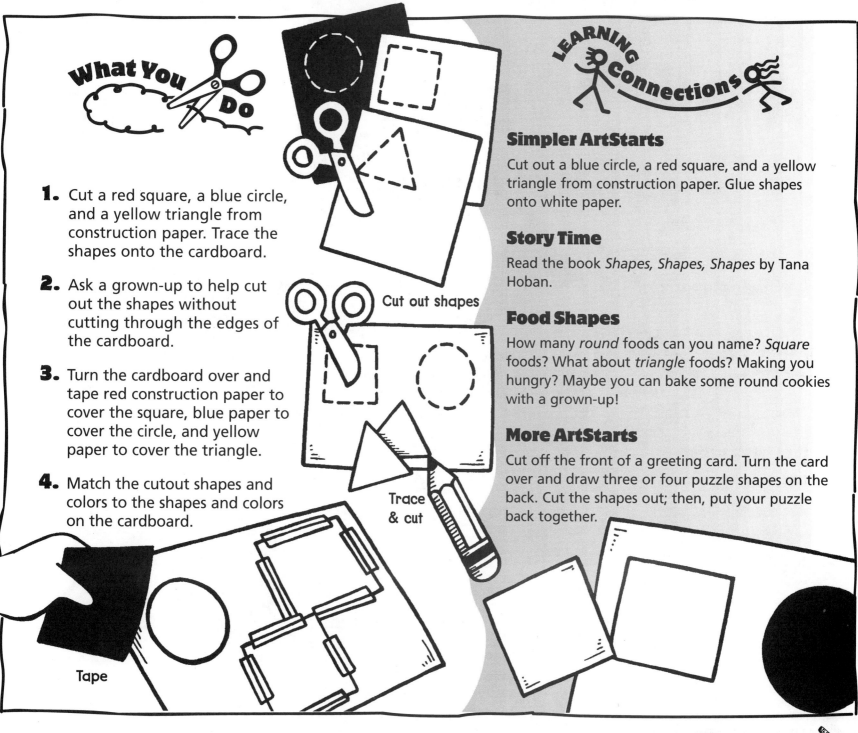

What You Do

1. Cut a red square, a blue circle, and a yellow triangle from construction paper. Trace the shapes onto the cardboard.

2. Ask a grown-up to help cut out the shapes without cutting through the edges of the cardboard.

3. Turn the cardboard over and tape red construction paper to cover the square, blue paper to cover the circle, and yellow paper to cover the triangle.

4. Match the cutout shapes and colors to the shapes and colors on the cardboard.

Cut out shapes

Trace & cut

Tape

LEARNING Connections

Simpler ArtStarts

Cut out a blue circle, a red square, and a yellow triangle from construction paper. Glue shapes onto white paper.

Story Time

Read the book *Shapes, Shapes, Shapes* by Tana Hoban.

Food Shapes

How many *round* foods can you name? *Square* foods? What about *triangle* foods? Making you hungry? Maybe you can bake some round cookies with a grown-up!

More ArtStarts

Cut off the front of a greeting card. Turn the card over and draw three or four puzzle shapes on the back. Cut the shapes out; then, put your puzzle back together.

Pinwheel Color Spin

Spin those colors,
red and blue,
Spin so fast
there's purple, too!

What You  Need

- **Child safety scissors**
- **White construction paper**
- **Red and blue markers**
- **Plastic drinking straw**
- **Hole punch**
- **Paper fastener***

*Note: Paper fasteners pose choking and poking danger to young children. Adults should control the supply and insert them into the project.

What You Do

Cut

1. Cut out a circle from white construction paper. Divide the circle into 12 wedges, like a pie cut into 12 pieces. Color one wedge blue, the next one red, the next blue, and so on, alternating the two colors.

2. Ask a grown-up to poke a hole in the center of the circle. Pinch the top of the straw flat. Punch a hole through the center of the flattened part of the straw.

Color

3. Ask a grown-up to attach the colored circle loosely to the straw with a paper fastener. Spin the circle. What new color do you see?

Attach & spin

Simpler ArtStarts

Dip one hand in a thin layer of red finger paint and press onto white paper for a handprint. Before it dries, dip the same hand in blue finger paint and press on top of the first handprint. Name the new color you've made.

Primary Color Mix

Red and blue are *primary colors*. Yellow is a primary color, too. Make a yellow and blue pinwheel. What color do you see when you spin it? What about a yellow and red pinwheel?

Story Time

Read the book *Mouse Paint* by Ellen Stoll Walsh.

Shades of Color

Finger-paint with tempera paints. What happens when you add white to a color? What happens when you add black to a color? Experiment to see what colors you can make.

Color Spin Game

Spin the arrow,
take your turn.
Having fun
while you learn!

What You Need

- Pencil
- Lid, deli or yogurt size, for tracing
- Large white paper plate
- Markers, any 4 colors
- Clip-on clothespins, 2
- Child safety scissors
- Black construction paper scrap
- Paper fastener*

What You Do

1. Trace the lid to make a circle in the center of the paper plate. Draw two lines, dividing the circle in four pieces like a pie. Color each section a different color.

2. Draw a ring around the rim of the plate. Divide the ring into 1" (2.5-cm) squares — about the size of half of your pointer finger. Color the squares the four different colors.

3. Write the words **Start** and **Finish** on two side-by-side squares. Write the players' names on the clothespins.

4. Cut an arrow shape from the black construction paper scrap. Ask a grown-up to attach the arrow with the fastener* to the center of the plate.

5. To play, take turns spinning the arrow. Clip the clothespin to the color square the arrow points to that's closest to the Start. Continue moving around the plate until one player reaches the Finish.

***Note:** Paper fasteners pose choking and poking danger to young children. Adults should control the supply and insert them into the project.

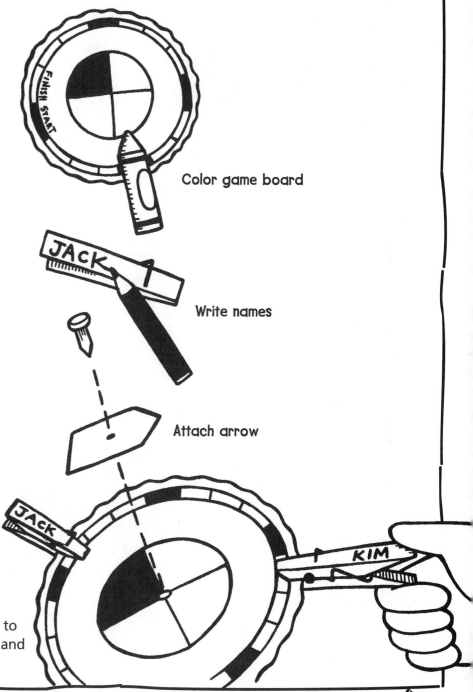

Color game board

Write names

Attach arrow

Simpler ArtStarts

Use markers to color clothespins different colors. Look for objects that are the same color as the clothespins. Clip the clothespin to the matching object.

Color Count

On a white piece of paper, color in a small square each time that color appears on the spinner. At the end of the game, count the number of squares of each color to see which ones the spinner chose the *most* and the *least*.

Color Walk

Go for a color walk outdoors. Gather leaves, berries, flowers, shells, and other natural finds. Sort all similar colors together. Are there different shades of each color? Sort each color group from the *lightest* to the *darkest*.

In My Garden

Lovely Ladybugs

A ladybug
is colored bright,
With black dots on
the left and right.

What You Need

- **Paper muffin cups**
- **Glue stick**
- **Light-colored construction paper**
- **Green and black markers**
- **Red tempera paint, in a small dish or lid**
- **Plastic bottle cap**

What You Do

1. To make the flowers, glue the muffin cups onto the construction paper. Use a green marker to draw on leaves and stems.

2. To make the ladybugs, dip the bottle cap into the paint. Then, press the cap onto the paper and muffin-cup flowers. Let dry.

3. Use a black marker to draw the ladybugs' wings, antennae, legs, and spots.

Draw

Dip

Print & draw

Learning Connections

Simpler ArtStarts

Cut out a large circle from red construction paper. Fold the paper in half; then, open it flat. Drip small dots of black paint onto one half of the circle. Refold the paper and rub gently; then open again. Where are the ladybug's dots now?

Math Starts

Count the number of ladybugs you printed on the paper. Now count all the dots. Which ladybug has the *most* dots? Which one has the *least* number of dots?

Symmetry

To make ladybug cookies, draw a line with a plastic knife down the center of each unbaked round cookie. Press an equal number of raisins or chocolate chips on each side, just like the dots on a ladybug. Look around indoors and out for other things that have two halves that look the same.

Science Starts

Ladybugs are *insects*, with antennae, six legs, and wings. Let a ladybug crawl on you and see if you can count its legs.

Funny Flower

Flowers of many colors
and many shapes, too.
Flowers to make you happy;
May I pick one for you?

- **Child safety scissors**
- **Construction paper, assorted colors**
- **White craft or tacky glue**
- **Plastic bottle cap**
- **Pom-pom**
- **Popsicle stick**
- **Green marker**

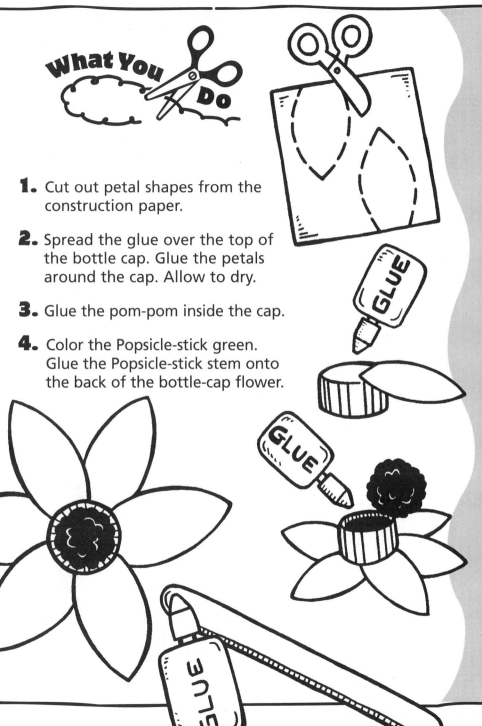

What You Do

1. Cut out petal shapes from the construction paper.

2. Spread the glue over the top of the bottle cap. Glue the petals around the cap. Allow to dry.

3. Glue the pom-pom inside the cap.

4. Color the Popsicle-stick green. Glue the Popsicle-stick stem onto the back of the bottle-cap flower.

Learning Connections

Simpler ArtStarts

Glue Popsicle sticks onto cardboard to make flower stems. Use markers to draw colorful flowers on top of the stems.

More ArtStarts

Make several flowers with Popsicle-stick stems. Ask a grown-up to cut slits in the lid of a shoe box. Place the lid back on the box and then press a Popsicle-stick flower into each slit. Or, glue a paper muffin cup to a Popsicle-stick. Glue seedpods or other natural finds into the cup.

Color Recognition

Take a walk in a garden or meadow with a grown-up. Name all the flower colors you see. Which color is your favorite?

Science & Nature

Plant a few sunflower seeds — one to each small paper cup filled with soil. Water gently. Place the cups in a sunny window. When the seeds sprout, plant them outdoors in your garden. Hello, sunshine!

Flying Paper Bird

Birds can fly
in the sky.
If they can
why can't I?

- **Small white paper plate**
- **Child safety scissors**
- **Yarn**
- **Tape**
- **Scrap brown paper**
- **Markers**

What You Do

Cut

1. Fold the paper plate in half; then, open it flat. Make wings by cutting along the inside circle on both sides of the plate, stopping before the fold line as shown.

2. Ask a grown-up to poke a small hole in the center of the fold. Tie a knot in the bottom of the yarn; then, thread the yarn up through the hole.

Tape sides

3. Fold the plate in half; tape it to hold. Cut a triangle beak from the scrap paper. Tape it in place.

Tape beak

4. Bend the wings outward. Color the bird with markers; then, hang it up to fly!

Color

Learning Connections

Simpler ArtStarts

Glue strips of brown construction paper onto a large white paper plate. Glue on leaves and dried grass to make a bird's nest.

Observe & Compare

Look for birds' nests in trees and bushes. What materials can you find outside that might make the nest *soft* or *sturdy*? Drape pieces of colorful yarn, ribbon, fabric, and lint outside for the birds; then, look for them in new nests!

Nature Starts

Search for bird footprints in the snow or in damp sand. Do they go in a straight line, a circle, or in a wavy line?

Listening Skills

Listen to the birds chirp and sing. Do you hear different patterns of chirps from different kinds of birds? Try imitating the sounds you hear — a bird may even answer you back!

Story Time

Read the book *The Mountain That Loved a Bird* by Alice McLerran.

The Carrot Patch

Nibble, nibble,
Is what you hear
When rabbits make carrots
Disappear!

What You Need

- **Green construction paper**
- **Child safety scissors**
- **Popsicle sticks, 4**
- **Orange, black, and brown markers**
- **White craft glue**
- **Cotton ball**

Fold & cut

Color

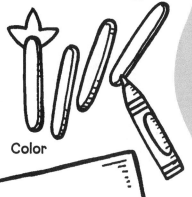

1. Fold the green construction paper in half; cut it into two pieces. Cut carrot tops from one half of the construction paper.

2. Color the Popsicle sticks orange. Glue the carrot tops onto the sticks.

3. With grown-up help, cut small slits in the other half of the construction paper. Insert the "carrots" into the slits. Draw a rabbit with black or brown markers. Glue a cotton ball to the paper for the rabbit's tail.

Math Starts

Count the number of carrots you "planted." How many carrots would be left if the hungry rabbit ate just one? (Remove one carrot from your patch to see.) What if the rabbit ate two carrots? How many carrots would you have if you planted two more?

Nature Starts

Ask a grown-up to cut off the top of a carrot that still has leaves. Put the carrot in water or on a wad of wet cotton. When new roots form, plant the carrot in soil. Water well. You'll soon have a bushy green plant to keep in your room!

With My Friends

Each person folds two large brown paper grocery bags flat. Squat down and step on the first bag. Place the second bag in front of you. Hop like a rabbit off the first bag and land on the second bag. Reach behind and place the first bag in front. Continue hopping on the bags until you cross the finish line. Hop-hop-hop!

Apple Tree

Pick some apples
from the tree
To make a pie
for you and me!

What You Need

- **Brown and green markers**
- **Popsicle sticks, 4**
- **Tacky glue**
- **Cereal-box cardboard**
- **Magnetic tape, 5 strips, each 4" (10 cm) long**
- **Child safety scissors**
- **Small red pom-poms**

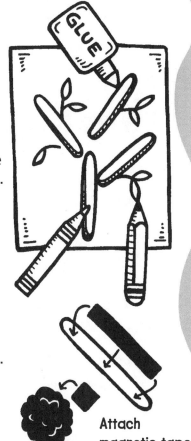

1. Color the Popsicle sticks brown. Glue one Popsicle stick onto the cardboard to make a tree trunk. Glue the remaining Popsicle sticks above the trunk to make branches. Draw leaves next to the branches.

2. Glue a strip of magnetic tape to each Popsicle-stick branch.

3. Cut the remaining strip of magnetic tape into small pieces. Glue a piece of magnetic tape onto each pom-pom to make apples. Place the apples on the Popsicle-stick branches.

Attach magnetic tape

Add apples

Fine Motor Skills

Attach small pieces of magnetic tape to red pom-poms. Attach pom-poms to a metal baking sheet or to the refrigerator door. Now, practice picking them off!

With My Friends

Make a second tree, so that you and a friend each have your own. Use another piece of magnetic strip to make a basket under each tree. The first player tosses a die and picks that number of apples off the tree and places them into the basket. Then the second person takes a turn. The first player to move all the apples from the tree to the basket wins!

Math Starts

Ask a grown-up to cut an apple in half. How many slices do you have? Cut each slice in half again. Now how many slices do you have? Can you put the apple back together?

Taste Sensations

Make a baked apple treat. Core an apple (do not cut all the way to the bottom) and then put some cinnamon, sugar, and butter in the center of the apple. Bake at 350°F (180°C) until it is done. Compare the taste and the texture (feeling on your tongue) of the baked apple and the fresh apple. Yum!

Spider Web

Spider, spider
in your web
catch your dinner,
then off to bed!

What You Need

- **Black tempera paint, in a small lid or dish**
- **Small white paper plate**
- **Black marker**
- **Child safety scissors**
- **Black thread**
- **Tape**

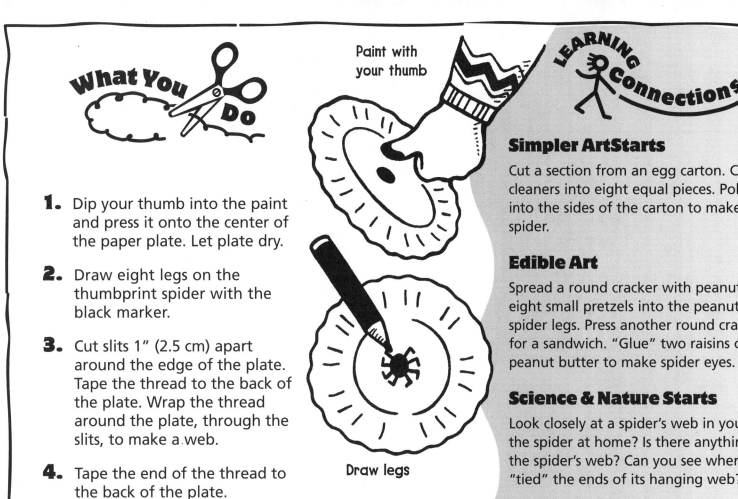

What You Do

Paint with your thumb

1. Dip your thumb into the paint and press it onto the center of the paper plate. Let plate dry.

2. Draw eight legs on the thumbprint spider with the black marker.

3. Cut slits 1" (2.5 cm) apart around the edge of the plate. Tape the thread to the back of the plate. Wrap the thread around the plate, through the slits, to make a web.

4. Tape the end of the thread to the back of the plate.

Draw legs

Simpler ArtStarts

Cut a section from an egg carton. Cut two pipe cleaners into eight equal pieces. Poke the stems into the sides of the carton to make a crawling spider.

Edible Art

Spread a round cracker with peanut butter. Press eight small pretzels into the peanut butter for spider legs. Press another round cracker on top for a sandwich. "Glue" two raisins on top with peanut butter to make spider eyes.

Science & Nature Starts

Look closely at a spider's web in your garden. Is the spider at home? Is there anything caught in the spider's web? Can you see where the spider "tied" the ends of its hanging web?

Make web & tape end of thread behind plate

Cut slits

Fluttering Butterfly

What's that I see
flitting by?
It's a butterfly
that I spy!

What You Need

- Pipe cleaners, 2
- Child safety scissors
- Tissue paper, any color
- Markers
- Transparent tape

What You Do

1. Cut one pipe cleaner in half. Twist half of the cut pipe cleaner around the top half of the uncut pipe cleaner.

2. Spread apart the tips of the two pipe cleaners to make butterfly antennae.

3. Cut out butterfly wings from the tissue paper. Decorate with markers. Place the pipe-cleaner body in the center of the wings. Tape to hold in place.

Twist

Decorate &
tape together

Simpler ArtStarts

Spread a thin layer of finger paint in a shallow tray. Place both hands in the paint. Press hands, with thumbs together and fingers touching, onto paper to make a butterfly print. Beautiful!

Science & Nature Starts

Butterflies are attracted to the colors *red* and *yellow*. Plant red and yellow flowers such as marigolds and zinnias to attract butterflies to your yard. How many butterflies do you see each day?

Story Time

Read the book *The Very Hungry Caterpillar* by Eric Carle. Now, imagine all those flying butterflies as crawling caterpillars!

Scrunch & Stretch

Can you move like a caterpillar? Lay flat on the ground; then, slide your knees to your chest. Stretch out flat again; then, slide your knees up again. Great crawling!

Dramatic Play

Cut an old sheet in half. Using one half sheet only, tie a corner around each wrist. Now, flutter away!

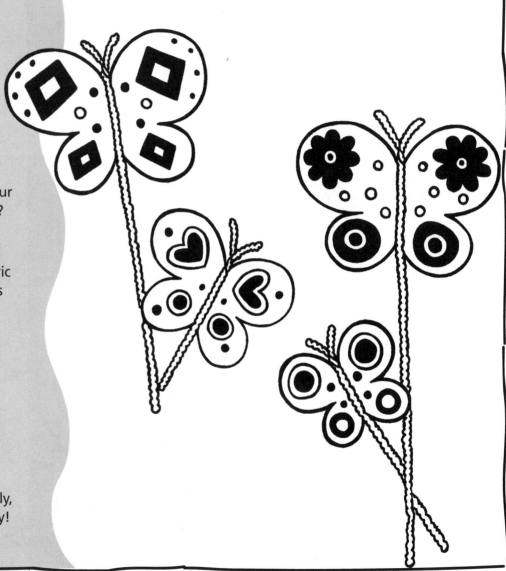

Blinking Fireflies

Firefly, firefly
awake at night.
How do you make
that flashing light?

What You Need

- Child safety scissors
- Black, green, and brown construction paper
- Glue
- Yellow tissue paper
- Hole punch
- Tape

What You Do

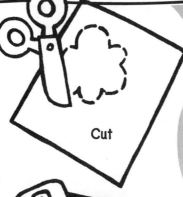

Cut

1. Cut out some trees, shrubs, and grass from the brown and green paper. Glue them onto the black paper.

2. For the fireflies, punch holes in the black paper. Turn the paper over and glue scraps of yellow tissue paper over the holes. Turn back over and hold up to the light to see the fireflies better.

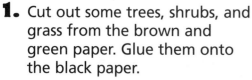

Glue

Punch holes

Simpler ArtStarts

Attach bright yellow sticker dots to black construction paper for fireflies.

More ArtStarts

Poke holes in the bottom of a paper cup and place the cup over a flashlight. Turn off the lights and aim the flashlight on a nearby wall. Move the flashlight back and forth. Can you see the "fireflies" flitting?

Nature Starts

Go outdoors on a summer evening with a grown-up. Look for fireflies around trees, shrubs, and grass. Can you see their twinkling lights? Gently cup your hands together to catch a firefly. Open up your hands slightly to peek at the firefly's light; then, release it and watch it fly away.

Secret Codes

Fireflies make flashing patterns that other fireflies can recognize. You can make up a flashing code, too! Use flashlights to signal a message to a friend. One flash could signal, "Hello." What other signals can you make up?

Stencil Stars

Pretty stars,
shining so bright.
So good to see you
twinkling tonight!

What You Need

- Pencil
- Paper plate
- Child safety scissors
- Blue construction paper
- Kitchen sponge
- White tempera paint, in a lid or dish

What You Do

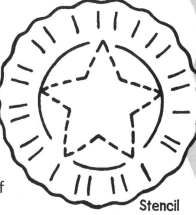
Stencil

1. Draw a star in the center of a paper plate. Cut out the star without cutting into the rim of the plate. (Ask a grown-up to help you get started.)

2. Hold the star stencil against the blue paper. Dip the sponge into the paint and dab it over the stencil.

Sponge on paint

3. Lift the star stencil and move it to another place on the blue paper. Repeat the paint dabbing. Repeat until the blue paper is covered with stars.

LEARNING Connections

Simpler ArtStarts

Cut a sponge in the shape of a star. Dip the sponge into a thin layer of white tempera paint. Press onto blue construction paper.

More ArtStarts

For sparkling stars, sprinkle silver glitter over each star while the paint is still wet.

The Night Sky

Design your own group of stars, called a *constellation*, with star stickers on black construction paper.

Math Starts

Write the numerals 1 to 10 on a sheet of paper. Place a matching number of star stickers next to each number

Rhyme & Sing

Sing or say as many songs or poems that you can think of that are about the moon or stars.

My Bedtime Book

Hop in bed
and say goodnight.
Close your eyes,
sweet dreams, sleep tight!

What You Need

- **Dark blue or black construction paper**
- **Stapler**
- **Drawing paper**
- **Markers**
- **Glue**

Fold & staple

1. Stack three or four sheets of construction paper together. Fold in half to make a book. Staple the folded edge.

2. Draw a picture of each special thing you do at night on separate pieces of paper. Number them in order, from the first thing you do to the last.

3. Glue them in your book in the order you do them. Now you have your very own bedtime story that you can read yourself!

Draw

Glue

Simpler ArtStarts

Glue bedtime pictures onto dark blue construction paper to make a bedtime collage.

Night Sounds

The sounds you hear at night can be very special. Listen to *outdoor sounds* in the night. Do you hear rain falling against the window? The church bell ringing the hour? Now listen to *indoor sounds* in the night. Do you hear a baby crying or a grown-up snoring?

Story Time

Read the book *Baby's Boat* by Jeanne Titherington.

Silvery Moon

Gentle moon, silvery moon,
way up in the sky;
Do you play with the stars
dancing right nearby?

What You Need

- **Child safety scissors**
- **Large white paper plate**
- **Aluminum foil**
- **Tape**
- **Blue crayon**
- **Star stickers**
- **Hole punch**
- **Thread**

What You Do

1. Cut out the center of the paper plate, without cutting through the rim. Then, cut a crescent moon shape from the center. Wrap the moon shape in foil; tape to hold.

2. Color the rim of the plate blue. Attach star stickers or tiny pieces of foil.

3. Punch a hole in the top of the moon. Cut notches in the top of the plate. Lace the thread through the hole in the moon; then, wrap it around the notches to hold it. Hold up the plate so the moon hangs down.

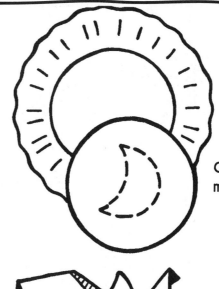

Cut out plate & moon shape

Wrap in foil

Cut

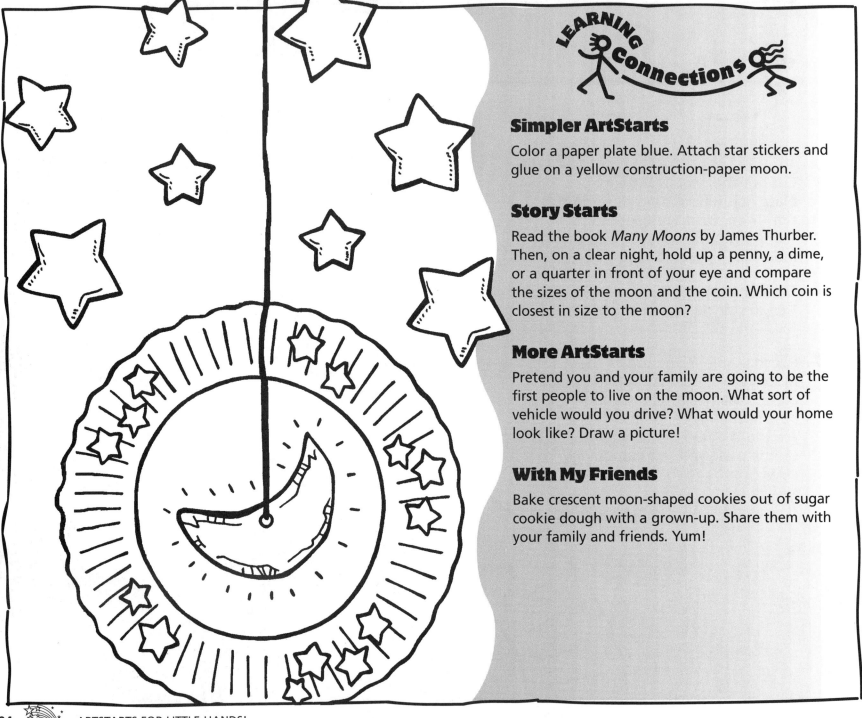

Simpler ArtStarts

Color a paper plate blue. Attach star stickers and glue on a yellow construction-paper moon.

Story Starts

Read the book *Many Moons* by James Thurber. Then, on a clear night, hold up a penny, a dime, or a quarter in front of your eye and compare the sizes of the moon and the coin. Which coin is closest in size to the moon?

More ArtStarts

Pretend you and your family are going to be the first people to live on the moon. What sort of vehicle would you drive? What would your home look like? Draw a picture!

With My Friends

Bake crescent moon-shaped cookies out of sugar cookie dough with a grown-up. Share them with your family and friends. Yum!

Matching Mittens

Mittens, mittens —
red, white, and blue;
Which pair of mittens
belongs to you?

What You Need

- Pencil
- Index cards
- Child safety scissors
- Gift-wrap paper, assorted patterns
- Glue stick
- Hole punch
- Yarn

What You Do

Draw & cut

1. Draw the shape of a mitten onto an index card. Cut it out.

2. Choose one pattern of gift wrap and glue it onto two index cards.

3. Trace the mitten shape onto the back of one card. Now, flip the mitten over and trace it onto the back of the second card. Cut out the pair of mittens.

4. Punch a hole in the bottom of each mitten. Thread the yarn through the holes and tie the mittens together.

Glue gift wrap

Trace & cut

Learning Connections

Simpler ArtStarts

Place your hands flat on a piece of construction paper. Ask a friend to trace around them. Decorate your mittens with markers.

Play Matching Mittens

Make several pairs of matching mittens. Instead of tying them together, turn the mittens pattern side down. Take turns flipping over any two mittens to find matching pairs. Remove matches; flip over mismatches. When all the pairs are matched, count how many pairs each player has.

Sock Sort

The next time the laundry is done, help to match the socks. Look for socks that are the same color, patterns, and size to make a perfect match. Good work!

Story Time

Read the book *The Mitten* by Jan Brett.

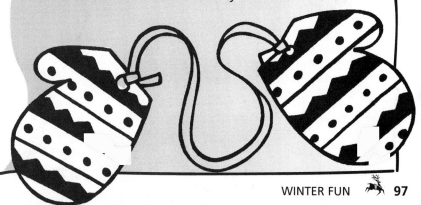

Snowy Pine Tree Mobile

Snow on pine trees;
what a beautiful sight.
Hang these trees
where they'll sparkle so bright!

What You Need

- **Green construction paper**
- **Child safety scissors**
- **Kitchen sponge**
- **White tempera paint, in lid or dish**
- **Plastic berry basket**
- **Brown marker**
- **Tape**
- **Yarn**
- **Pipe cleaner**

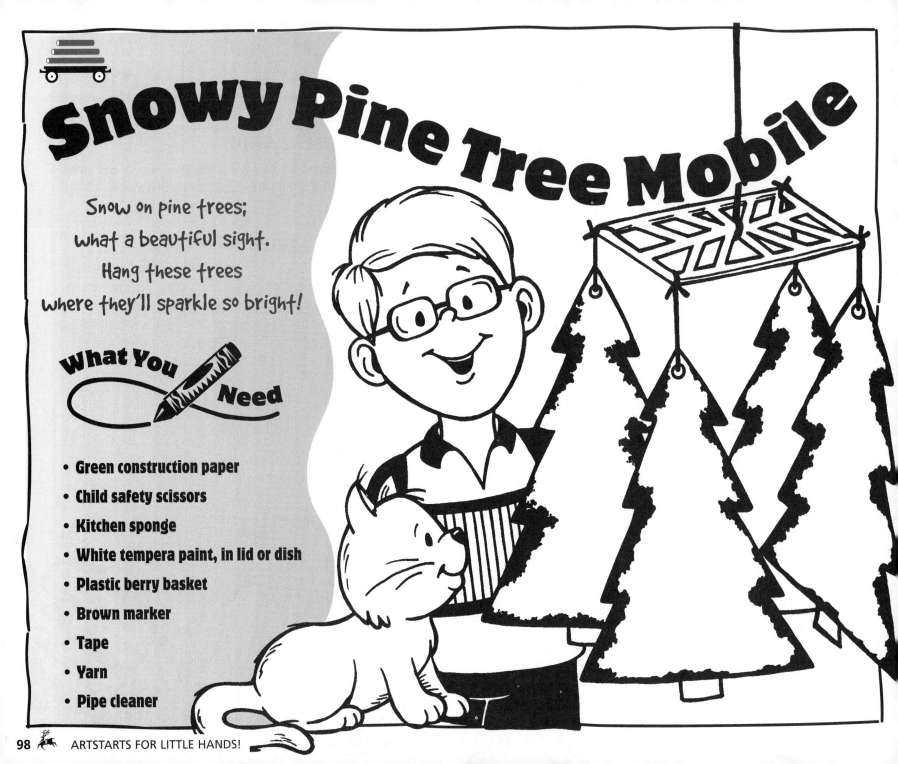

What You Do

1. Fold green construction paper in half. Cut a jagged line along the unfolded edge to make a pine-tree shape. Unfold the paper. Make several of these pine trees.

2. Dip a sponge in white paint and dab onto the trees for snow.

3. Cut away the sides of a berry basket. Dab the bottom with white paint. Let dry.

4. Color the tree trunks brown. Tape yarn to the trees and tie it to the basket bottom. Twist the pipe cleaner through the center of the basket to make a hanger for your mobile.

Fold & cut

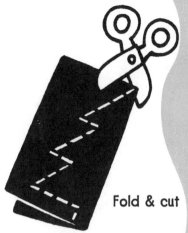

Sponge-paint

Cut basket bottom

Learning Connections

More ArtStarts

For sparkling trees, outline the pine trees with white craft glue. Sprinkle glitter onto the glue; then, shake off the excess.

Winter Party

Draw a winter scene for some party invitations. Make pine-tree mobiles for decorations. Cut out sandwiches in rounds to look like snowballs and serve frosted tree-shaped cookies and ice cream for dessert.

Language Starts

Make a word chain. Draw circles on a paper and ask a grown-up to write all the winter words you can think of — one in each circle.

Snowy Footprints

Who is walking
across the snow?
Make some footprints;
then you'll know!

What You  Need

- **Kitchen sponge**
- **White tempera paint,
  in dish or lid**
- **Black construction paper,
  2 sheets**
- **Child safety scissors**
- **Glue stick**

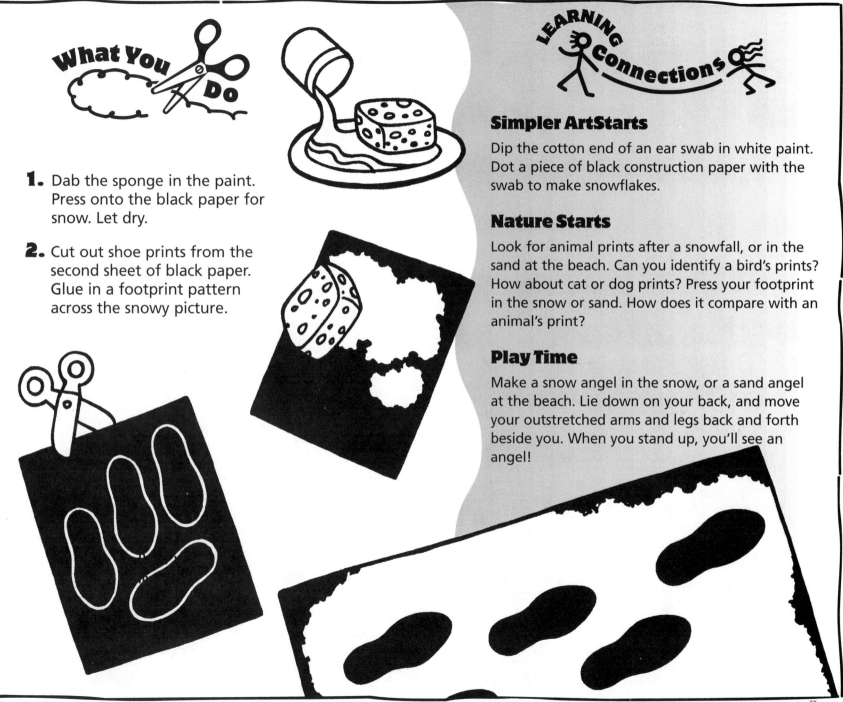

What You Do

1. Dab the sponge in the paint. Press onto the black paper for snow. Let dry.

2. Cut out shoe prints from the second sheet of black paper. Glue in a footprint pattern across the snowy picture.

LEARNING Connections

Simpler ArtStarts

Dip the cotton end of an ear swab in white paint. Dot a piece of black construction paper with the swab to make snowflakes.

Nature Starts

Look for animal prints after a snowfall, or in the sand at the beach. Can you identify a bird's prints? How about cat or dog prints? Press your footprint in the snow or sand. How does it compare with an animal's print?

Play Time

Make a snow angel in the snow, or a sand angel at the beach. Lie down on your back, and move your outstretched arms and legs back and forth beside you. When you stand up, you'll see an angel!

Snowy Day Scene

When you're drawing a winter scene
and need some snow to fall,
Try tissue paper and glue;
see, it's not hard at all!

What You Need

- **Child safety scissors**
- **Small white paper plates, 2**
- **Transparent tape**
- **Clear plastic wrap**
- **White tissue paper**
- **White craft glue**
- **Markers**

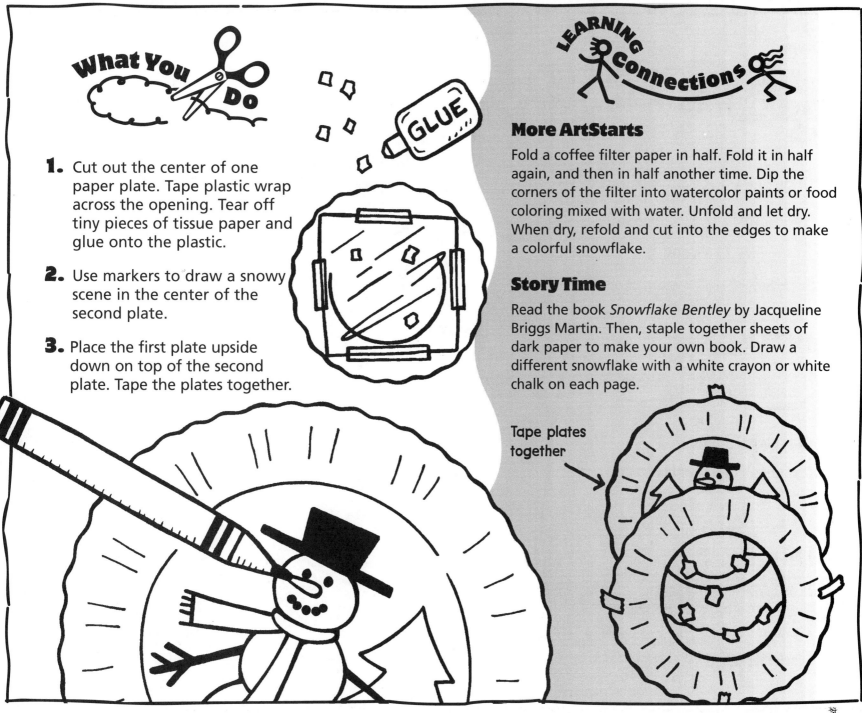

What You Do

1. Cut out the center of one paper plate. Tape plastic wrap across the opening. Tear off tiny pieces of tissue paper and glue onto the plastic.

2. Use markers to draw a snowy scene in the center of the second plate.

3. Place the first plate upside down on top of the second plate. Tape the plates together.

GLUE

Learning Connections

More ArtStarts

Fold a coffee filter paper in half. Fold it in half again, and then in half another time. Dip the corners of the filter into watercolor paints or food coloring mixed with water. Unfold and let dry. When dry, refold and cut into the edges to make a colorful snowflake.

Story Time

Read the book *Snowflake Bentley* by Jacqueline Briggs Martin. Then, staple together sheets of dark paper to make your own book. Draw a different snowflake with a white crayon or white chalk on each page.

Tape plates together

Fluffy snowman

Build a snowman
Dressed in hat, scarf, and belt.
Enjoy it today
'Cause tomorrow it may melt!

What You Need

- **Child safety scissors**
- **Cereal-box cardboard, 2 large pieces**
- **White craft glue**
- **Blue construction paper**
- **Cotton balls**
- **Black and orange tissue-paper scraps**
- **Black marker**

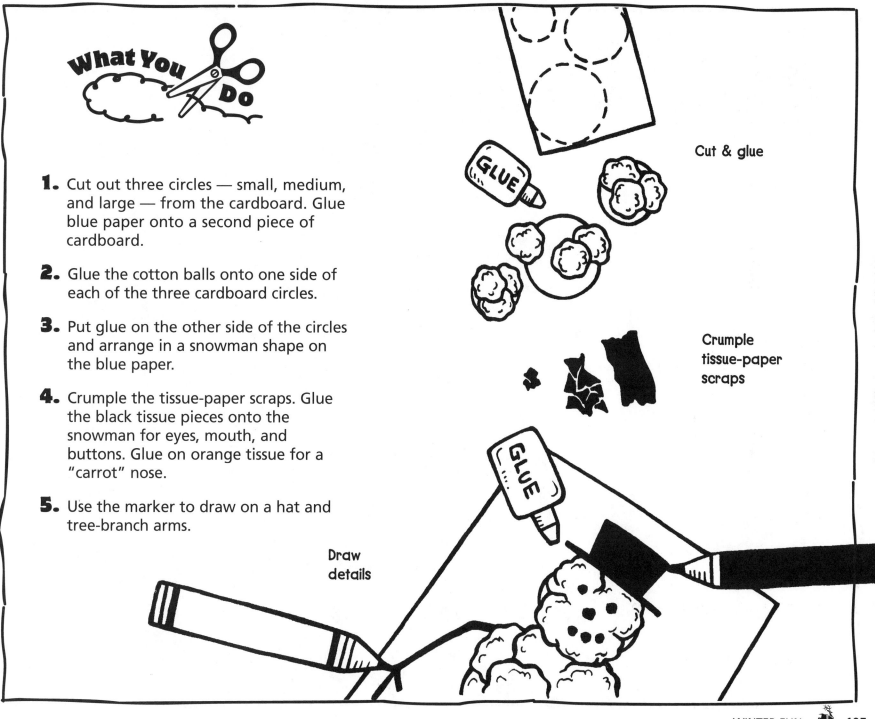

What You Do

1. Cut out three circles — small, medium, and large — from the cardboard. Glue blue paper onto a second piece of cardboard.

2. Glue the cotton balls onto one side of each of the three cardboard circles.

3. Put glue on the other side of the circles and arrange in a snowman shape on the blue paper.

4. Crumple the tissue-paper scraps. Glue the black tissue pieces onto the snowman for eyes, mouth, and buttons. Glue on orange tissue for a "carrot" nose.

5. Use the marker to draw on a hat and tree-branch arms.

GLUE

Cut & glue

Crumple
tissue-paper
scraps

GLUE

Draw
details

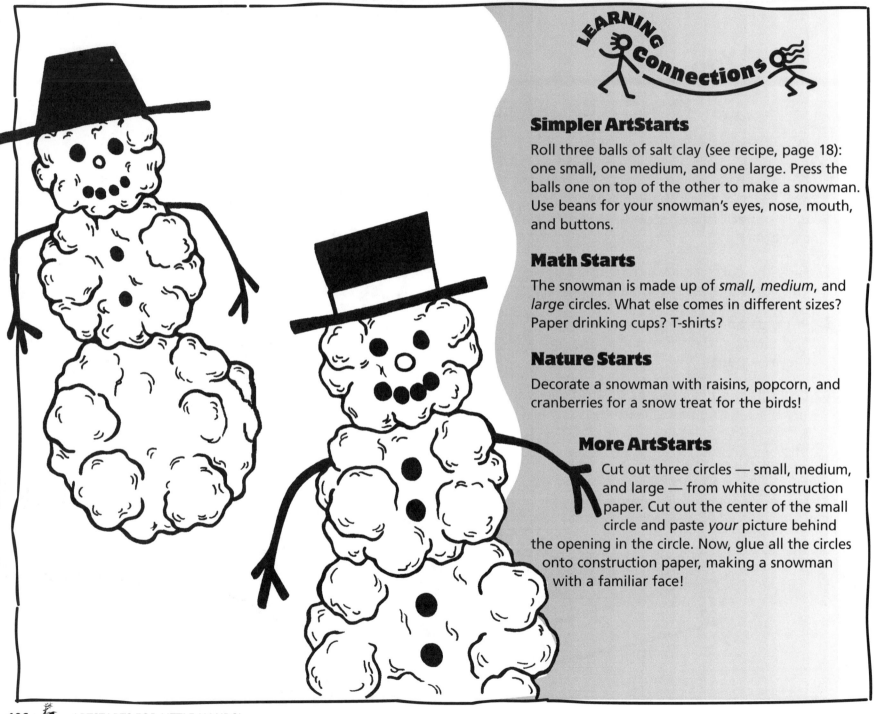

LEARNING Connections

Simpler ArtStarts

Roll three balls of salt clay (see recipe, page 18): one small, one medium, and one large. Press the balls one on top of the other to make a snowman. Use beans for your snowman's eyes, nose, mouth, and buttons.

Math Starts

The snowman is made up of *small, medium*, and *large* circles. What else comes in different sizes? Paper drinking cups? T-shirts?

Nature Starts

Decorate a snowman with raisins, popcorn, and cranberries for a snow treat for the birds!

More ArtStarts

Cut out three circles — small, medium, and large — from white construction paper. Cut out the center of the small circle and paste *your* picture behind the opening in the circle. Now, glue all the circles onto construction paper, making a snowman with a familiar face!

Mix Up, Match Up

Pictures of kids
just like you.
Just spin and mix;
then, match them, too!

What You Need

- **Child safety scissors**
- **Old magazines or catalogs**
- **White paper plates, 1 large & 1 small**
- **Paper fastener***
- **Glue**

***Note:** Paper fasteners pose choking and poking danger to young children. Adults should control the supply and insert them into the project.

What You Do

Cut

1. Cut out (or draw) pictures of kids that will fit on the plate from old magazines. Cut each picture in half.

2. Ask a grown-up to attach the plates in the center with the small plate on top.

3. Glue the bottom halves of the pictures, with feet facing toward the center, around the rim of the small plate. Glue the top halves of the pictures along the rim of the large plate.

4. Spin the smaller plate to mix and match the pictures.

Fasten

Learning Connections

Simpler ArtStarts

Make matching cards by cutting out people and animal pictures from old magazines. Glue each picture onto an index card. Cut each card in half. Place the cards face up, mix them up, and match the cards back together.

Half & Whole

Plan a "half" meal with a friend. Each person eats half a sandwich, half a carrot, and drinks half a glass of milk. Still hungry? Make another half meal to fill you the *whole* way up!

Lace-Up Shoes

Look at this,
what a sight!
These old shoes
are tied just right!

What You Need

- Pencil
- Shoes, various sizes
- Cereal-box cardboard
- Child safety scissors
- Hole punch
- Markers or crayons
- Yarn
- Tape

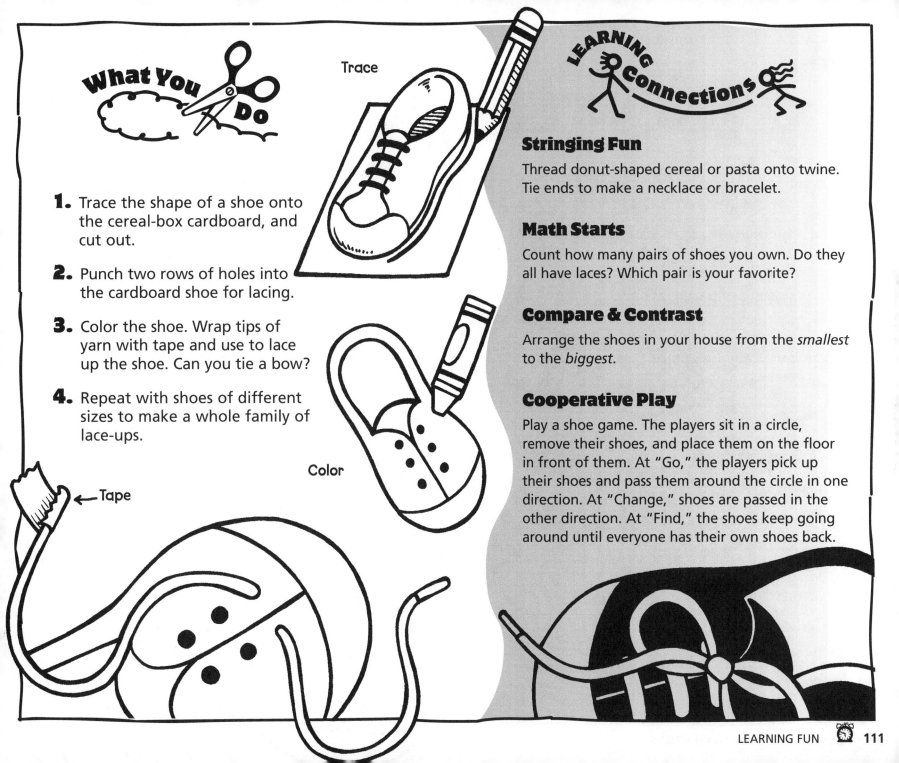

What You Do

Trace

1. Trace the shape of a shoe onto the cereal-box cardboard, and cut out.

2. Punch two rows of holes into the cardboard shoe for lacing.

3. Color the shoe. Wrap tips of yarn with tape and use to lace up the shoe. Can you tie a bow?

4. Repeat with shoes of different sizes to make a whole family of lace-ups.

Color

← Tape

LEARNING Connections

Stringing Fun

Thread donut-shaped cereal or pasta onto twine. Tie ends to make a necklace or bracelet.

Math Starts

Count how many pairs of shoes you own. Do they all have laces? Which pair is your favorite?

Compare & Contrast

Arrange the shoes in your house from the *smallest* to the *biggest*.

Cooperative Play

Play a shoe game. The players sit in a circle, remove their shoes, and place them on the floor in front of them. At "Go," the players pick up their shoes and pass them around the circle in one direction. At "Change," shoes are passed in the other direction. At "Find," the shoes keep going around until everyone has their own shoes back.

Playful Puppets

It's time for
a puppet show;
Have them dance
and say, "Hello!"

What You Need

- **Child safety scissors**
- **Styrofoam plate**
- **Tape**
- **Popsicle sticks, 2**
- **Construction paper, assorted colors**
- **Tacky glue**
- **Wiggly eyes**
- **Pipe cleaners, 2**

What You Do

Back of head

1. For the puppet's face, cut out a circle from the center of the plate.

2. For the body, tape the two Popsicle sticks end to end. Tape one end to the back of the puppet's head.

3. Fold a piece of construction paper in half and cut out a T-shape for the puppet's costume. Cut a small slit in the top of the fold and insert the end of the Popsicle stick. Glue the costume closed.

4. Cut out the puppet's nose, mouth, ears, and hands from paper; glue on. Glue on the wiggly eyes. Add cutout paper buttons, a bow tie, or other clothes.

5. Cut the pipe cleaners into pieces. To make hair, poke the ends around the top edge of the face, and twist them.

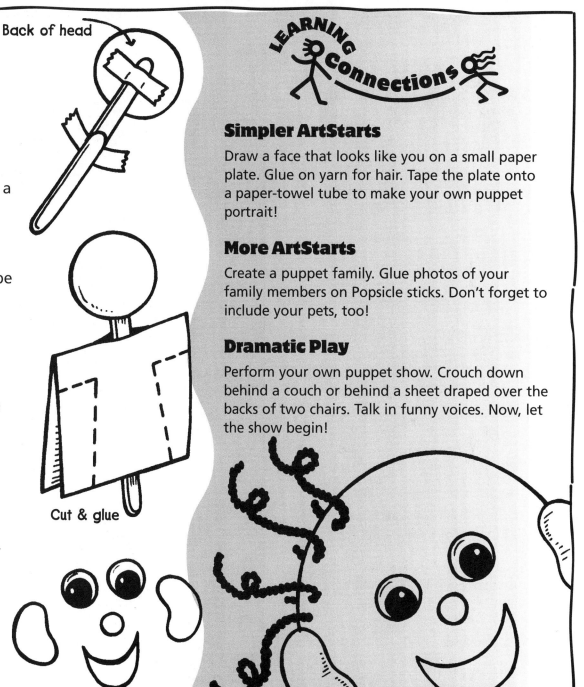

Cut & glue

LEARNING Connections

Simpler ArtStarts

Draw a face that looks like you on a small paper plate. Glue on yarn for hair. Tape the plate onto a paper-towel tube to make your own puppet portrait!

More ArtStarts

Create a puppet family. Glue photos of your family members on Popsicle sticks. Don't forget to include your pets, too!

Dramatic Play

Perform your own puppet show. Crouch down behind a couch or behind a sheet draped over the backs of two chairs. Talk in funny voices. Now, let the show begin!

Tick-Tock Clock

Hooray! Hooray!
It's time to play!
This clock keeps time
All through the day.

What You Need

- Pencil
- Clear plastic deli lid
- Construction paper, a light-colored sheet, plus scraps of black
- Child safety scissors
- Black marker
- Paper fastener*

***Note:** Paper fasteners pose choking and poking danger to young children. Adults should control the supply and insert them into the project.

What You Do

Trace

1. Trace the deli lid onto the light paper. Cut out the paper circle, making the circle slightly smaller than the outline, so it will fit inside the lid for the face of the clock.

2. With grown-up help, write the numbers 1 to 12 in clockwise order around the outside edge of the circle to show the clock's hours. Place the clock face into the lid.

Write numbers

3. Cut two arrows for the clock's hands from the black construction paper scraps. Make one hand long (the minute hand) and one hand short (the hour hand).

4. Ask a grown-up to attach the hands to the front of the lid and through the clock face with a paper fastener.

5. Point the clock's hands to tell the time!

Cut & assemble

Simpler ArtStarts

With grown-up help, write the numbers 1 to 12 around the rim of a large white paper plate, cut out the clock's hands from black paper, and attach them to the plate with a paper fastener. Move the hands of the clock to tell what time you go to bed. Read *Bedtime For Frances* by Russell Hoban.

More ArtStarts

Ask a grown-up to poke a hole on opposite sides of the deli lid. Tie elastic sewing tape through the holes to make a watchband. Now, wear your "super-sized" watch on your wrist!

Math Starts

Count how many clocks are in your house or classroom. Are they all the *same* or can you find *different* kinds of clocks?

Snack Time!

Make muffins with a grown-up. Help set the timer for the baking time; then, when they're done, sit down for "snack time!"

Music Shaker

Tum-te-dum-dum,
de-deet-de-deet
Shake and dance
as you keep the beat!

What You Need

- **Round cardboard carton with lid (oatmeal, cornmeal, or breadcrumb containers)**
- **Dried beans or seeds**
- **Masking tape**
- **Markers**
- **Brown paper lunch bag**

What You Do

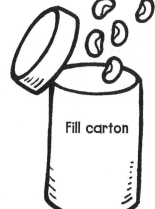

Fill carton

1. Fill the empty carton with dried beans or seeds; replace the lid and tape shut.

2. Use markers to decorate both sides of the bag.

Decorate bag

3. Put the carton inside the lunch bag. Fold down the top of the lunch bag; tape it flat. Gather the bag on the sides of the carton; tape them flat.

4. Give your new music maker a shake. Let the dancing begin!

Tape & shake

Learning Connections

Simpler ArtStarts

Fill an empty margarine tub or deli container with dried beans or seeds. Tape the lid on tightly. Play some music and shake the container to the beat.

More ArtStarts

Tape crepe-paper streamers to the ends of your music maker. Put on some music. Wave and shake.

Making Music

Tape two or three round cardboard cartons together to make drums. Use a wooden spoon to beat out a rhythm. Play some music and follow the beat. What other sounds can you add? Give an instrument to everyone in your family and strike up a family band!

Science Starts

Fill drinking glasses with water at different levels. Gently tap the rim of each glass with a spoon. What do you notice about the water level and the sounds? Why do you think that happens?

Activity Index By Skill Level

Check the symbol at the beginning of each activity to quickly assess the challenge level.

Easy for even the littlest hands.

Colorful Circles, 54
Key Ring, 36
Matching Mittens, 96
My Bedtime Book, 90
Popsicle Stick Match, 56
Runaway Balloons, 22
Sandy Island, 28
School of Fish, 10
Snowy Footprints, 100
Sunshine Wand, 30

Mix Up, Match Up, 108
Music Shaker, 116
Perky Hat, 32
Pinwheel Color Spin, 64
Salt Clay Mouse, 16
Silvery Moon, 92
Spider Web, 80
Stencil Stars, 88
Stop & Go!, 44
Terrific Turtles, 2
Tick-Tock Clock, 114
Tissue-Paper Sun Catchers, 26

Require a few steps.

Bird in a Cage, 6
Blinking Fireflies, 86
The Carrot Patch, 76
Circus Train, 48
Color Sort, 58
Colored Puzzle Shapes, 62
Cuckoo Bird Mask, 8
Easy Elephant, 12
Fluffy Snowman, 104
Fluttering Butterfly, 82
Funny Flower, 72
Goofy Glasses, 24
In the Car, 42
Lace-Up Shoes, 110
Lovely Ladybugs, 70

More advanced projects.

Apple Tree, 78
Back-Seat Drivers, 38
Brown Bear Puppet, 14
Bus Ride, 40
Choo-Choo Train, 50
Flying Paper Bird, 74
Kitty Cat, 4
Color Spin Game, 56
Playful Puppets, 112
Racing Cars, 46
Rainbow Mobile, 60
Snowy Day Scene, 102
Snowy Pine Tree Mobile, 98
Super Sailboats, 20

More Good Books
from
W Williamson Publishing Co.

Williamson books are available from your bookseller or directly from Williamson Publishing.
Please see the last page for ordering information or to visit our website. Thank you.

More Williamson Books By Judy Press!

**AROUND-THE-WORLD
ART & ACTIVITIES**
Visiting the 7 Continents through Craft Fun
Ages 3 to 7, 144 pages, fully illustrated, trade paper,
10 x 8, $12.95
A Williamson *Little Hands*® Book

• *Parent's Guide Children's Media Award*
ALPHABET ART
With A to Z Animal Art & Fingerplays
Ages 2 to 6, 144 pages, fully illustrated, trade paper,
10 x 8, $12.95.
A Williamson *Little Hands*® Book

• *Real Life Award*
• *Children's Book-of-the-Month Club Main Selection*
THE LITTLE HANDS ART BOOK
Exploring Arts & Crafts with 2- to 6-Year-Olds
160 pages, fully illustrated, trade paper,
10 x 8, $12.95.
A Williamson *Little Hands*® Book

• *Parents' Choice Approved*
THE LITTLE HANDS BIG FUN CRAFT BOOK
Creative Fun for 2- to 6-Year-Olds
144 pages, fully illustrated, trade paper,
10 x 8, $12.95.
A Williamson *Little Hands*® Book

• *Early Childhood News Directors' Choice Award*
• *Real Life Award*
VROOM! VROOM!
Making 'dozers, 'copters, trucks & more
Ages 4 to 10, 160 pages, fully illustrated, trade paper,
11 x 8 1/2, $12.95
A Williamson *Kids Can!*® Book

THE KIDS' NATURAL HISTORY BOOK
Making Dinos, Fossils, Mammoths & More
Ages 4 to 10, 144 pages, fully illustrated, trade paper,
11 x 8 1/2, $12.95
A Williamson *Kids Can!*® Book

Little Hands® Books . . .
SETTING THE STAGE FOR LEARNING!
- **Build early learning skills**
- **Support all learning styles**
- **Promote self-esteem**

The following *Little Hands®* books for ages 2 to 7 are each 144 pages, fully illustrated, trade paper, 10 x 8, $12.95 US.

WOW! I'M READING!
Fun Activities to Make Reading Happen
by Jill Frankel Hauser

THE LITTLE HANDS PLAYTIME! BOOK
50 Activities to Encourage Cooperation & Sharing
by Regina Curtis

- *Early Childhood News Directors' Choice Award*
- *Parents' Choice Approved*
- *Parent's Guide Children's Media Award*

SCIENCE PLAY!
Beginning Discoveries for 2- to 6-Year-Olds
by Jill Frankel Hauser

- *American Bookseller Pick of the Lists*

RAINY DAY PLAY!
Explore, Create, Discover, Pretend
by Nancy Fusco Castaldo

- *Parents' Choice Gold Award*
- *Children's Book-of-the-Month Club Selection*

FUN WITH MY 5 SENSES
Activities to Build Learning Readiness
by Sarah A. Williamson

- *Early Childhood News Directors' Choice Award*
- *Parents' Choice Approved*

SHAPES, SIZES & MORE SURPRISES!
A Little Hands Early Learning Book
by Mary Tomczyk

- *Parents' Choice Approved*

THE LITTLE HANDS NATURE BOOK
Earth, Sky, Critters & More
by Nancy Fusco Castaldo

MATH PLAY!
80 Ways to Count & Learn
by Diane McGowan and Mark Schrooten